Test Yourself

Research Methods and Design in Psychology

Test Yourself... Psychology Series

Test Yourself

Research Methods and Design in Psychology

Dominic Upton and Penney Upton

Multiple-Choice Questions prepared by Laura Scurlock-Evans

LearningMatters

First published in 2011 by Learning Matters Ltd

British Library Cataloguing in Publication Data
A CIP record for this book is available from the British Library

ISBN: 978 0 85725 665 2

This book is also available in the following e-book formats:
Adobe ebook ISBN: 978 0 85725 667 6
ePUB book ISBN: 978 0 85725 666 9
Kindle ISBN: 978 0 85725 668 3

Cover design by Toucan Design
Text design by Toucan Design
Project Management by Deer Park Productions, Tavistock, Devon
Typeset by Pantek Media, Maidstone, Kent
Printed and bound in Great Britain by MPG Books Group, Bodmin, Cornwall

Learning Matters Ltd
20 Cathedral Yard
Exeter
EX1 1HB
Tel: 01392 215560
info@learningmatters.co.uk
www.learningmatters.co.uk

Contents

Acknowledgements

The production of this series has been a rapid process with an apparent deadline at almost every turn. We are therefore grateful to colleagues both from Learning Matters (Julia Morris and Helen Fairlie) and the University of Worcester for making this process so smooth and (relatively) effortless. In particular we wish to thank our colleagues for providing many of the questions, specifically:

- Biological Psychology: Emma Preece
- Cognitive Psychology: Emma Preece
- Developmental Psychology: Charlotte Taylor
- Personality and Individual Differences: Daniel Kay
- Research Methods and Design in Psychology: Laura Scurlock-Evans
- Social Psychology: Laura Scurlock-Evans

Finally, we must, once again, thank our children (Gabriel, Rosie and Francesca) for not being as demanding as usual during the process of writing and development.

Introduction

Psychology is one of the most exciting subjects that you can study at university in the twenty-first century. A degree in psychology helps you to understand and explain thought, emotion and behaviour. You can then apply this knowledge to a range of issues in everyday life including health and well-being, performance in the workplace, education – in fact any aspect of life you can think of! However, a degree in psychology gives you much more than a set of 'facts' about mind and behaviour; it will also equip you with a wide range of skills and knowledge. Some of these, such as critical thinking and essay writing, have much in common with humanities subjects, while others such as hypothesis testing and numeracy are scientific in nature. This broad-based skill set prepares you exceptionally well for the workplace – whether or not your chosen profession is in psychology. Indeed, recent evidence suggests employers appreciate the skills and knowledge of psychology graduates. A psychology degree really can help you get ahead of the crowd. However, in order to reach this position of excellence, you need to develop your skills and knowledge fully and ensure you complete your degree to your highest ability.

This book is designed to enable you, as a psychology student, to maximise your learning potential by assessing your level of understanding and your confidence and competence in research methods and design in psychology, one of the core knowledge domains for psychology. It does this by providing you with essential practice in the types of questions you will encounter in your formal university assessments. It will also help you make sense of your results and identify your strengths and weaknesses. This book is one part of a series of books designed to assist you with learning and developing your knowledge of psychology. The series includes books on:

- Biological Psychology
- Cognitive Psychology
- Developmental Psychology
- Personality and Individual Differences
- Research Methods and Design in Psychology
- Social Psychology

In order to support your learning this book includes over 200 targeted Multiple-Choice Questions (MCQs) and Extended Multiple-Choice Questions (EMCQs) that have been carefully put together to help assess your depth of knowledge of research methods and design in psychology. The MCQs are split into two formats: the foundation level questions are about your level of understanding of the key principles and components of key areas in psychology. Hopefully, within these questions you should recognise the correct answer from the four options. The advanced level questions require more than simple recognition – some will require recall of key information, some will require application of this information and others will require synthesis of information. At the end of each chapter you will find a set of essay questions covering each of the topics. These are typical of the kinds of question that you are likely to encounter during your studies. In each chapter, the first essay question is broken down for you using a concept map, which is intended to help you develop a detailed answer to the question. Each of the concept maps is shaded to show you how topics link together, and includes cross-references to relevant MCQs in the chapter. You should be able to see a progression in your learning from the foundation to the advanced MCQs, to the extended MCQs and finally the essay questions. The book is divided up into 11 chapters and your research methods and design in psychology module is likely to have been divided into similar topic areas. However, do not let this restrict your thinking in relation to research methods and design in psychology: these topics interact. The sample essay questions, which complement the questions provided in the chapter, will help you to make the links between different topic areas. You will find the answers to all of the MCQs and EMCQs at the end of the book. There is a separate table of answers for each chapter; use the self monitoring column in each of the tables to write down your own results, coding correct answers as NC, incorrect answers as NI and any you did not respond to as NR. You can then use the table on page 115 to analyse your results.

The aim of the book is not only to help you revise for your exams, it is also intended to help with your learning. However, it is not intended to replace lectures, seminars and tutorials, or to supersede the book chapters and journal articles signposted by your lecturers. What this book can do, however, is set you off on a sound footing for your revision and preparation for your exams. In order to help you to consolidate your learning, the book also contains tips on how to approach MCQ assessments and how you can use the material in this text to assess, *and enhance*, your knowledge base and level of understanding.

Now you know the reasons behind this book and how it will enhance your success, it is time for you to move on to the questions – let the fun begin!

Assessing your interest, competence and confidence

The aim of this book is to help you to maximise your learning potential by assessing your level of understanding, confidence and competence in core issues in psychology. So how does it do this?

Assessing someone's knowledge of a subject through MCQs might at first glance seem fairly straightforward: typically the MCQ consists of a question, one correct answer and one or more incorrect answers, sometimes called distractors. For example, in this book each question has one right answer and three distractors. The goal of an MCQ test is for you to get every question right and so show just how much knowledge you have. However, because you are given a number of answers to select from, you might be able to choose the right answer either by guessing or by a simple process of elimination – in other words by knowing what is not the right answer. For this reason it is sometimes argued that MCQs only test knowledge of facts rather than in-depth understanding of a subject. However, there is increasing evidence that MCQs can also be valuable at a much higher level of learning, if used in the right way (see, for example, Gardner-Medwin and Gahan, 2003). They can help you to develop as a self-reflective learner who is able to recognise the interest you have in a subject matter as well as your level of competence and confidence in your own knowledge.

MCQs can help you gauge your interest, competence and confidence in the following way. It has been suggested (Howell, 1982) that there are four possible states of knowledge (see Table 1). Firstly, it is possible that you do not know something and are not aware of this lack of knowledge. This describes the naive learner – think back to your first week at university when you were a 'fresher' student and had not yet begun your psychology course. Even if you had done psychology at A level, you were probably feeling a little self-conscious and uncertain in this new learning environment. During the first encounter in a new learning situation most of us feel tentative and unsure of ourselves; this is because we don't yet know what it is we don't know – although to feel this lack of certainty suggests that we know there is something we don't know, even if we don't yet know what this is! In contrast, some people appear to be confident and at ease even in new learning situations; this is not usually because they already know everything but rather because they too do not yet know what it is they do not know – but they have yet to even acknowledge that there is a gap in their knowledge. The next step on from this 'unconscious non-competence' is 'conscious non-competence'; once you started your psychology course you began to realise what the gaps were in your knowledge – you now knew what you didn't know! While this can be an uncomfortable feeling, it is important for the learning process that this acknowledgement of a gap in knowledge is made, because it is the first step in reaching the next level of learning – that of a 'conscious competent' learner. In other words you need to know what the gap in your knowledge is so that you can fill it.

Table 1 Consciousness and competence in learning

	Unconscious	Conscious
Non-competent	You don't know something and are not aware that you lack this knowledge/skill.	You don't know something and are aware that you lack this knowledge/skill.
Competent	You know something but are not aware of your knowledge/skill.	You know something and are aware of your knowledge/skill.

One of the ways this book can help you move from unconscious non-competency to conscious competency should by now be clear – it can help you identify the gaps in your knowledge. However, if used properly it can do much more; it can also help you to assess your consciousness and competence in this knowledge.

When you answer an MCQ, you will no doubt have a feeling about how confident you are about your answer: 'I know the answer to question 1 is A. Question 2 I am not so sure about. I am certain the answer is not C or D, so it must be A or B. Question 3, I haven't got a clue so I will say D – but that is a complete guess.' Sound familiar? Some questions you know the answers to, you have that knowledge and know you have it; other questions you are less confident about but think you may know which (if not all) are the distractors, while for others you know this is something you just don't know. Making use of this feeling of confidence will help you become a more reflective – and therefore effective – learner.

Perhaps by now you are wondering where we are going with this and how any of this can help you learn. 'Surely all that matters is whether or not I get the answers right? Does that show I have knowledge?' Indeed it may well do and certainly, if you are confident in your answers, then yes it does. But what if you were not sure? What if your guess of D for our fictional question 3 above was correct? What if you were able to complete all the MCQs in a test and score enough to pass – but every single answer was a guess? Do you really know and understand psychology because you have performed well – and will you be able to do the same again if you retake the test next week? Take a look back at Table 1. If you are relying on guesswork and hit upon the answer by accident you might perform well without actually understanding how you know the answer, or that you even knew it (unconscious competence), or you may not realise you don't know something (unconscious non-competence). According to this approach to using MCQs what is important is not how many answers you get right, but whether or not you acknowledge your confidence in the answer you give: it is better to get a wrong answer and acknowledge it is wrong (so as to work on filling that gap).

Therefore what we recommend you do when completing the MCQs is this: for each answer you give, think about how confident you are that it is right. You might want to rate each of your answers on the following scale:

3:     I am confident this is the right answer.

2:     I am not sure, but I think this is the right answer.

1:     I am not sure, but I think this is the wrong answer.

0:     I am confident this is the wrong answer.

Using this system of rating your confidence will help you learn for yourself both what you know and what you don't know. You will become a conscious learner through the self-directed activities contained in this book. Reflection reinforces the links between different areas of your learning and knowledge and strengthens your ability to *justify* an answer, so enabling you to perform to the best of your ability.

References

Gardner-Medwin, A.R. and Gahan, M. (2003) *Formative and Summative Confidence-Based Assessment*, Proceedings of 7th International Computer-Aided Assessment Conference, Loughborough, UK, July, pp. 147–55.

Howell, W.C. (1982) 'An overview of models, methods, and problems', in W.C. Howell and E.A. Fleishman (eds), *Human performance and productivity, Vol. 2: Information processing and decision making.* Hillsdale, NJ: Erlbaum.

Tips for success: how to succeed in your assessments

This book, part of a comprehensive new series, will help you achieve your psychology aspirations. It is designed to assess your knowledge so that you can review your current level of performance and where you need to spend more time and effort reviewing and revising material. However, it hopes to do more than this – it aims to assist you with your learning so it not only acts as an assessor of performance but as an aid to learning. Obviously, it is not a replacement for every single text, journal article, presentation and abstract you will read and review during the course of your degree programme. Similarly, it is in no way a replacement for your lectures, seminars or additional reading – it should complement all of this material. However, it will also add something to all of this other material: learning is assisted by reviewing and assessing and this is what this text aims to do – help you learn through assessing your learning.

The focus throughout this book, as it is in all of the books in this series, is on how you should approach and consider your topics in relation to assessment and exams. Various features have been included to help you build up your skills and knowledge ready for your assessments.

This book, and the other companion volumes in this series, should help you learn through testing and assessing yourself – it should provide an indication of how advanced your thinking and understanding is. Once you have assessed your understanding you can explore what you need to learn and how. However, hopefully, quite a bit of what you read here you will already have come across and the text will act as a reminder and set your mind at rest – you do know your material.

Succeeding at MCQs

Exams based on MCQs are becoming more and more frequently used in higher education and particularly in psychology. As such you need to know the best strategy for completing such assessments and succeeding. The first thing to note is, if you know the material then the questions will present no problems – so revise and understand your notes and back this up with in-depth review of material presented in textbooks, specialist materials and journal articles. However, once you have done this you need to look at the technique for answering multiple-choice questions and here are some tips for success:

1. Time yourself. The first important thing to note when you are sitting your examination is the time available to you for completing it. If you have, for example, an hour and a half to answer 100 multiple-choice questions this means you have 54 seconds to complete each question. This means that you have to read, interpret, think about and select one answer for a multiple-choice question in under a minute. This may seem impossible, but there are several things that you can do to use your time effectively.

2. Practise. By using the examples in this book, those given out in your courses, in class tests, or on the web you can become familiar with the format and wording of multiple-choice questions similar to those used in your exam. Another way of improving your chances is to set your own multiple-choice exams – try and think of some key questions and your four optional responses (including the correct one of course!). Try and think of optional distractors that are sensible and not completely obvious. You could, of course, swap questions with your peers – getting them to set some questions for you while you set some questions for them. Not only will this help you with your practice but you will also understand the format of MCQs and the principles underlying their construction – this will help you answer the questions when it comes to the real thing.

3. The rule of totality. Look out for words like 'never' and 'always' in multiple-choice questions. It is rare in psychology for any answer to be true in relation to these words of 'totality'. As we all know, psychology is a multi-modal subject that has multiple perspectives and conflicting views and so it is very unlikely that there will always be a 'never' or an 'always'. When you see these words, focus on them and consider them carefully. A caveat is, of course, sometimes never and always will appear in a question, but be careful of these words!

4. Multiple, multiple-choice answers. Some multiple-choice answers will contain statements such as 'both A and C' or 'all of the above' or 'none of these'. Do not be distracted by these choices. Multiple-choice questions have only one correct answer and do not ask for opinion or personal bias. Quickly go through each choice independently, crossing off the answers that you know are not true. If, after eliminating the incorrect responses, you think there is more than one correct answer, group your answers and see if one of the choices matches yours. If you believe only one answer is correct, do not be distracted by multiple-choice possibilities.

5. 'First guess is best' fallacy. There is a myth among those who take (or even write) MCQs that the 'first guess is best'. This piece of folklore is misleading: research (and psychologists love research) indicates that when people change their answers on an MCQ exam, about two-thirds of the time they go from wrong to right, showing that the first guess is often not the best. So, think about it and consider your answer – is it right? Remember, your first guess is not better than a result obtained through good, hard, step-by-step, conscious thinking that enables you to select the answer that you believe to be the best.

6. The rule of threes. One of the most helpful strategies for multiple-choice questions is a three-step process:

(i) Read the question thoroughly but quickly. Concentrate on particular words such as 'due to' and 'because' or 'as a result of' and on words of totality such as 'never' or 'always' (although see rule 3 above).

(ii) Rather than going to the first answer you think is correct (see rule 5) eliminate the ones that you think are wrong one by one. While this may take more time, it is more likely to provide the correct answer. Furthermore, answer elimination may provide a clue to a misread answer you may have overlooked.

(iii) Reread the question, as if you were reading it for the first time. Now choose your answer from your remaining answers based on this rereading.

7. Examine carefully. Examine each of the questions carefully, particularly those that are very similar. It may be that exploring parts of the question will be useful – circle the parts that are different. It is possible that each of the alternatives will be very familiar and hence you must **understand the meaning** of each of the alternatives with respect to the context of the question. You can achieve this by studying for the test as though it will be a short-answer or essay test. Look for the level of **qualifying words**. Such words as *best, always, all, no, never, none, entirely, completely* suggest that a condition exists without exception. Items containing words that provide for some level of exception or qualification are: *often, usually, less, seldom, few, more* and *most* (and see rule 3). If you know that two or three of the options are correct, **'all of the above'** is a strong possibility.

8. Educated guesses. Never leave a question unanswered. If nothing looks familiar, pick the answer that seems most complete and contains the most information. Most of the time (if not all of the time!) the best way to answer a question is to know the answer! However, there may be times when you will not know the answer or will not really understand the question. There are three circumstances in which you should guess: when you are stuck, when you are running out of time, or both of these! Guessing strategies are always dependent on the scoring system used to mark the exam (see the section on MCQ scoring mechanisms). If the multiple-choice scoring system makes the odds of gaining points equal to the odds of having points deducted it does not pay to guess if you are unable to eliminate any of the answers. But the odds of improving your test score are in your favour if you can rule out even one of the answers. The odds in your favour increase as you rule out more answers in any one question. So, take account of the scoring mechanisms and then eliminate, move onwards and guess!

9. Revise and learn. Study carefully and learn your material. The best tip for success is always to learn the material. Use this book, use your material, use your time wisely but, most of all, use your brain!

Chapter 1
Research in psychology

This chapter will test your knowledge of why research is conducted in psychology and includes questions on what is meant by the terms 'paradigm', 'epistemology' and 'ontology' and why these are crucial to understanding different approaches to research. Other topics covered include nomothetic, idiographic and hermeneutic research, qualitative research approaches, the scientific method, the role of hypotheses and the quantitative–qualitative research debate.

Select one of the possible answers for each question.

Foundation level questions

1. Which of the following is a myth about psychological research?

    A. Research is the collection of facts. ✓

    B. The gold standard of research is the experimental method. ✓

    C. Researchers in psychology always aim to be objective. ✓

    D. All of the above.

    Your answer: D ✓

2. Which of the following lists contains examples of different levels of explanation which are all appropriate for psychological research?

    A. Cultural, historical, socio-political and interpersonal.

    B. Cognitive, social, behavioural and developmental.

    C. Biological, neurological, physiological and evolutionary.

    D. All of the above.

    Your answer: D ✓

3. Epistemology is a branch of philosophy that is concerned with what?

A. The scientific method.

B. Theories of knowing and knowledge.

C. The meaning of truth.

D. The nature of existence.

Your answer: C ✗ B

4. Which of the following terms is not associated with the scientific method?

A. Hypothetico-deductive.

B. Positivism.

C. Empiricism.

D. Constructivism.

Your answer: C ✗ D

5. Merton (1967) suggested that there are two different types of theory. What did he call them?

A. Abstract and concrete.

B. Grand and mundane.

C. Grand and middle-range.

D. Structural and functional.

Merton
> grand & middle range

Your answer: A ✗ C

6. Early Gestalt psychological theories and research are an example of which approach?

A. Constructionism.

B. Reductionism.

C. Realism.

D. None of the above.

Gestalt → Reductionism

Your answer: C ✗ B

?

7. According to Kuhn, the collective set of attitudes, values, procedures and techniques that form the accepted perspective of a particular discipline at a specific point in time is called what?

   A. A paradigm.

   B. A philosophy.

   C. An epistemology.

   D. An ontology.

Kuhn - paradigm

Your answer: A ✓

8. Research that is interested in identifying the symbols people use to convey meaning in life, and how people interpret experiences is called what?

   A. Nomothetic.

   B. Idiographic.

   C. Hermeneutic.

   D. None of the above.

Symbols → hermeneutic

Your answer: B ✗ C

9. With which branch of psychology is the idiographic approach to research most commonly associated?

   A. Social psychology.

   B. Cognitive psychology.

   C. Individual differences.

   D. Biopsychology.

Idiographic approach Ind. diffs.

Your answer: A ✗ C

10. Which approach to research did Kurt Lewin propose in the 1940s?

   A. Ethnography.

   B. Endogenous research.

   C. Action research.

   D. Collaborative research.

Kurt Lewin → Action research

Your answer: A ✗ C

Advanced level questions

11. Which epistemological approach's heritage includes Weber's *Verstehen*, the hermeneutic-phenomenological tradition and symbolic interactionism?

A. Interpretivism.

B. Realism.

C. Ethnography.

D. Relativism.

Your answer: A ✓

Weber

12. What is a circular hypothesis?

A. A hypothesis which is not adequately defined.

B. A hypothesis which attempts to encompass too many concepts and is therefore untestable.

C. A hypothesis in which an event itself is used as the explanation of the event.

D. A hypothesis which posits that behaviour is cyclical.

Your answer: C ✓

13. The statement 'Teachers working in secondary education will score higher on a self-rated measure of stress than teachers working in primary education' is an example of what?

A. A directional hypothesis.

B. A theory.

C. A non-directional hypothesis.

D. A null hypothesis.

Your answer: A ✓

positivism?

14. Historically, with which branch of psychology is positivism most closely associated?

A. Cognitive.

B. Behaviourism.

C. Social.

D. Biopsychology.

Your answer: B ✓

15. Kidder and Fine (1987) proposed a distinction between research incorporating non-numerical data into _____ research designs, which they termed _____ research, and research based on open-ended, _____ research methodologies, focusing on theory generation and the exploration of meaning, which they termed _____ research.

kidder+fine (87)

   A. Small q, inductive, big Q, hypothetico-deductive.

Big Q /

   B. Hypothetico-deductive, small q, inductive, big Q.

   C. Small-scale, inductive, large-scale, hypothetico-deductive.

Small Q?

   D. Inductive, small-scale, hypothetico-deductive, large-scale.

Your answer: B ✓

16. Reflecting on the ways in which our own values, experience and beliefs, shape research is known as what?

   A. Personal reflexivity. *Personal reflexivity*

   B. Empirical reflexivity.

   C. Critical reflexivity.

   D. Epistemological reflexivity.

Your answer: C ✗ A

17. Which position, prominent in the natural sciences, argues that human experience and social behaviour can only be understood by reducing phenomena down to observable facts and examining the mathematical relationships between them?

   A. Empiricism.

   B. Inductivism.   *Positivism definition*

   C. Positivism.

   D. Rationalism.

Your answer: A ✗ C

18. Epistemological and ontological considerations have implications for which of the following?

A. Whether the focus in research is placed on internal or external factors as the driving force affecting behaviour.

B. The conception of and degree of emphasis placed on generalisability of research findings.

C. The research methodology used to explore phenomena.

D. All of the above.

Your answer: A X D   ontology

19. Allport (1939) argued that psychology should be viewed as a science and evaluated by its success in enhancing 'our powers of *predicting*, *understanding*, and *controlling* human action' above the levels achieved by what?

A. Chance.

B. Common sense.

Allport (1939)

C. Popularity.

D. None of the above.

Your answer: A <

20. Researchers in psychology have identified that merely *conducting* research can alter participants' behaviour. Which of the following terms reflects the phenomenon whereby features of an experimental setting bias participants to behave in particular ways?

A. The Hawthorne effect.

B. Social desirability effect.

C. Demand characteristics.

D. Social facilitation effect.

Your answer: B ✓ x B

Extended multiple-choice question

Complete the following paragraph using the items listed below. Not all of the items will be consistent with the paragraph and not all items can be used. Items can be used only once.

Although there is no single 'qualitative approach' to psychological research, many proponents of qualitative approaches argue that traditional quantitative methods conduct research in sterile conditions, often seeking to isolate people from their _____ in an attempt to ensure that all factors other than those of interest are _____. This can lead to _____ results and narrow theories, and because traditional quantitative methods seek to reduce social phenomena to _____, many qualitative researchers argue that they cannot capture the entirety of human experience. Some qualitative researchers also argue that because traditional quantitative methods seek to test hypotheses generated from prior theory rather than _____ through new research, this may actually stifle the development of new perspectives in psychology.

Optional items

A. generating hypotheses

B. proving relationships

C. social contexts

D. excessive

E. held constant

F. observed

G. artificial

H. sterile

I. numerical relationships

J. families

K. descriptions

L. working routines

M. fabricated

N. testing hypotheses

O. manipulated

Essay questions for Chapter 1

Once you have completed the MCQs above you are ready to tackle some essay questions. You might like to select three or four topics and make notes on them. One way of doing this is to create a concept map. The first question has been done for you and you can see how the knowledge required links to some of the MCQs in this chapter.

1. To what extent is psychology a science? Critically discuss from both quantitative and qualitative research perspectives.

2. Using examples from both quantitative and qualitative research, evaluate the position that quantitative research produces narrow and artificial theories.

3. To what extent does the paradigm within which a psychologist operates influence their research? Discuss, providing examples of research to illustrate your answer.

4. 'Psychological research should aim to apply the scientific method to social behaviour and phenomena in the same way that it is applied in the natural sciences.' Critically discuss this position, providing relevant evidence to support your argument.

5. Critically discuss the position that in psychology, nomothetic research which aims to identify universal laws governing psychological and social phenomena provides more meaningful results than those produced through idiographic or hermeneutic research. Provide relevant examples of theory to illustrate your answer.

6. Kurt Lewin argued that more research should be undertaken to address practical issues occurring in the everyday social world, to promote change. To what extent do you feel that action research should be the *standard* of research in psychology?

7. 'Day after day social scientists go out into the world. Day after day they discover that people's behaviour is pretty much what you'd expect' (Murphy, 1995). Using relevant examples, discuss the claim that psychological research adds no more to our understanding of social phenomena than using a 'common-sense' approach.

8. Allport often argued that 'psychology will become more scientific' if it embraces idiographic methodology. Critically evaluate this position.

9. Some researchers in psychology argue that quantitative and qualitative methodologies in research are mutually exclusive and cannot be combined in any meaningful way. Critically discuss this position providing evidence for your argument.

10. Critically describe and discuss how philosophical approaches have shaped the development and study of psychology.

Chapter 1 essay question 1: concept map

To what extent is psychology a science? Critically discuss from both quantitative and qualitative research perspectives.

The concept map below provides an example of how the first sample essay may be conceptualised. Consideration of the different epistemological and ontological positions underpinning different research perspectives leads to several subtopics, which should be critically evaluated before conclusions can be drawn. In this case the evidence suggests that understanding the different approaches' representations of reality (i.e. objective or subjective), directly influences the conceptualisation of psychological phenomena and the choice of methods adopted to explore them. Therefore, the extent to which psychology is viewed as a science or not is likely to differ depending on whether the quantitative or qualitative research perspective is adopted.

Remember that it is important to link your answers to other topic areas not covered in this chapter.

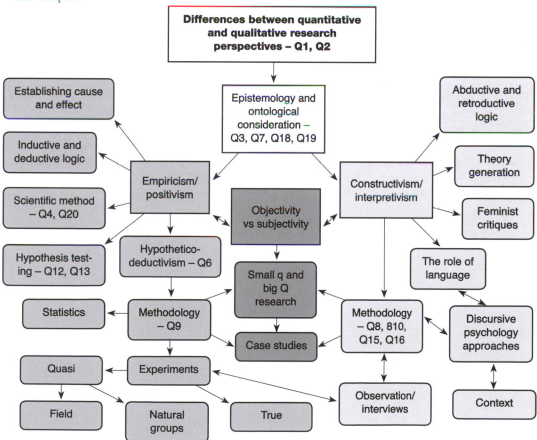

Chapter 2
Designing research studies

This chapter includes questions on issues which affect research design decisions, including levels of measurement, sources of data, sampling methods, types of variable, statistical analysis techniques, measures of central tendency, techniques used to avoid confounds and factors affecting choices of psychometric tests.

Select one of the possible answers for each question.

Foundation level questions

1. Complete the following sentence: 'Confounding variables are a problem in what?'

   A. Experimental studies.

   B. Longitudinal studies.

   C. Correlational studies.

   D. All of the above.

   Your answer: D ✓

2. The concept of 'variables', as used in psychology, originated from which discipline?

   A. Sociology.

   B. Statistics.

   C. Biology.

   D. There is no way of tracing its origins.

   Your answer: B ✓

3. The theory of measurement and scales of measurement were first introduced in psychology by whom?

   A. Binet.

   B. Skinner.

   C. Stanley.

   D. James.

   Your answer: B ✗ C

4. Which of the following lists contains all four levels of measurement?

    A. Nominal, dichotomous, ordinal, ratio.

    B. Nominal, ordinal, interval, ratio.

    C. Nominal, dichotomous, polynomial, ratio.

    D. Dichotomous, ordinal, interval, ratio.

Your answer: B ✓

5. A variable which *facilitates* the relationship between two variables is known as what?

    A. A mediator variable.

    B. A moderator variable.

    C. An extraneous variable.

    D. A confounded variable.

mediation /moderation

Your answer: A ✓

6. Why are research questions used in psychological research?

    A. They help guide a researcher to the topic which they would most enjoy studying.

    B. They guide a researcher's decisions about what data to collect and where this data should be collected from.

    C. They help guide a researcher's decisions to ensure their research is ecologically valid.

    D. All of the above.

Your answer: B ✓

7. Which of the following defines a probability sample or true random sample?

    A. Every unit in the population under investigation (e.g. people) has a known, equal probability of being selected.

    B. Ten per cent, or more, of the target population under investigation is recruited in the research.

    C. Every subgroup (e.g. class group) within the population is represented.

    D. Every unit in the population is sampled.

Your answer: A ✓

8. The method of sampling which involves identifying different levels or subgroups within a population (based on such things as employment type, educational level and political groups) from which a proportion of the population can then be randomly selected is known as what?

    A. Quota sampling.

    B. Opportunistic sampling.

    C. Stratified sampling.   *Types of Sampling.*

    D. Cluster sampling.

    Your answer: [A] × C

9. Which of the following lists contains sources of information which Parker (1992) suggested were suitable for Foucauldian discourse analysis?

    A. Speech, written text, advertisements.   *Sociology*

    B. Braille, Morse code, semaphore.

    C. Non-verbal behaviour, artwork, fashion-systems.

    D. All of the above.

    Your answer: [A] D ✓

10. When using psychometric tests in research, the administrator of the test is usually required to observe a set of procedures for its administration, scoring techniques and interpretation. What term is commonly used for this process?

    A. Establishing validity.

    B. Establishing reliability.

    C. Standardisation.

    D. Benchmarking.

    Your answer: [A] B × C

Advanced level questions

11. Cialdini, Reno and Kallgren (1990) wanted to explore the effect evidence of littering on a path had on people's willingness to litter. They handed leaflets to people who were about to walk down a path (in a park). On this path the researchers would have already put either 0, 1, 2, 4, 8 or 16 pieces of rubbish. Cialdini et al. then recorded whether people dropped their leaflet (littered) or not. What type of research design is this?

    A. Quasi-experiment.

    B. Laboratory experiment.

    C. Systematic observation.

    D. None of the above.

Your answer: C   ✗ A

12. What are the four different types of interview question outlined by Spradley (1979)?

    A. Open, closed, basic, rich.

    B. Explicative, formative, comparing, summary.

    C. Descriptive, structural, contrast, evaluative.

    D. Expressive, anatomical, abstract, integrating.

Your answer: C   ✓

13. Which sampling method is most commonly used in interpretative phenomenological analysis?

    A. Convenience.

    B. Purposive.

    C. Stratified random.

    D. Random.

Your answer: B   ✓

14. Ideally, if a study aims to assess whether caffeine consumption causes anxiety, it would have to do what?

   A. Randomly assign participants to groups of high and low caffeine consumption and compare their anxiety.

   B. Show a correlation between caffeine consumption and anxiety in participants.

   C. Measure caffeine consumption and anxiety over a period of time on at least two intervals.

   D. Any of the above.

Your answer: D   x A

15. In statistical analysis, which of the following techniques could be employed to examine mediated and moderated relationships?

   A. T-tests.

   B. Path analysis.

   C. Factor analysis.

   D. None of the above.

Design for med+mod
Path analysis
multiple levels high/low etc

Your answer: C

16. Football shirt numbers, women's dress sizes and the Fahrenheit temperature scale are examples of which three different levels of measurement? Choose the correct list from the following options.

ordinal   interval   ratio

   A. Ordinal, interval and ratio level data.

   B. Nominal, ordinal and ratio level data.

   C. Nominal, interval and ratio level data.

   D. Nominal, ordinal and interval level data.

example list of measurement types

Your answer: A   x D

17. The central tendency of a nominal variable is given by what?

   A. Mean.

   B. Median.

   C. Mode.

   D. Any of the above.

categorical

Your answer: B A X C

18. When designing qualitative research, 'critical language awareness' is an aspect of what?

   A. Reporting style.

   B. Researching reflexivity.

   C. Selecting texts for discourse analysis.

   D. None of the above.

Your answer: B ✓

19. What is a 'subject variable'?

   A. A variable that is manipulated by the researcher which is a characteristic of the participant.

   B. A variable that is not manipulated by the researcher but is a characteristic of the participant.

   C. A variable that is measured to see if it changes after another variable is manipulated.

   D. None of the above.

Your answer: A ✗ B

20. When choosing a psychometric test for use in a research project, which of the following would provide evidence of its validity?

   A. Strong correlations between the psychometric test you are interested in and another measure also aiming to assess the construct of interest.

   B. Internal consistency as measured using Cronbach's alpha. - Reliability measure

   C. Asking researchers in the field of the topic of interest whether the questionnaire is representative of the subject it is intended to cover.

   D. Both A and C.

Your answer: B ✗ D

→ use Birkbeck research module!
→ use slides from Amber.

Extended multiple-choice question

Complete the following paragraph using the items listed below. Not all of the items will be consistent with the paragraph and not all items can be used. Items can be used only once.

When designing a research study in psychology a key issue, particularly for _____ research, is _____. This refers to the degree to which the results of the study would be found again if the research was repeated. If results are replicated, we can have greater _____ that the psychological effect revealed by the research is _____. In order to be able to replicate a piece of research, the _____ details of the original study are required. This includes ensuring that all the _____, _____ and _____ obtained in the study are clearly stated in the _____. Otherwise, it is not possible to repeat the research without the risk of severely _____ the research findings, for example through using different procedures or techniques.

Optional items

A. confidence

B. of interest

C. quantitative

D. real

E. research report

F. limiting

G. full

H. qualitative

I. predictions

J. methods

K. replicability

L. results

M. confounding

Essay questions for Chapter 2

Once you have completed the MCQs above you are ready to tackle some essay questions. You might like to select three or four topics and make notes on them. One way of doing this is to create a concept map. The first question has been done for you and you can see how the knowledge required links to some of the MCQs in this chapter.

1. Critically discuss the role of theory in the research process, including examples of both quantitative and qualitative approaches.

2. What are the crucial differences between an experimental design and a correlation design? Critically evaluate their strengths and weaknesses, providing examples of contemporary psychological research.

3. Describe and evaluate the concept of standardisation and why it is important in psychological research.

4. Compare and evaluate experimental and survey research designs on the reliability and validity issues they face. How can these issues be managed?

5. Describe and evaluate the strengths and weaknesses of the longitudinal research study approach. How can this form of research be designed most effectively?

6. Critically discuss the ways in which the topic a researcher is interested in can shape the research's study design? Illustrate your answer using examples of contemporary psychological research.

7. Critically examine the ways in which an exploratory research project may be designed differently to a research study that seeks to test extant theory.

8. Discuss the implications of ethical considerations for psychologists when designing research studies. Provide examples of contemporary and/or classic research to illustrate your answer.

Chapter 2 essay question 1: concept map

Critically discuss the role of theory in the research process, including examples of both quantitative and qualitative approaches.

The concept map below provides an example of how the first sample essay may be conceptualised. Consideration of the different representations of reality (i.e. objective or subjective) leads to several subtopics, which should be critically evaluated before conclusions can be drawn. In this case exploring the similarities and differences between the aims, scope and methodologies of quantitative and qualitative approaches can help to shed light on the role of theory in research.

Remember that it is important to link your answers to other topic areas not covered in this chapter.

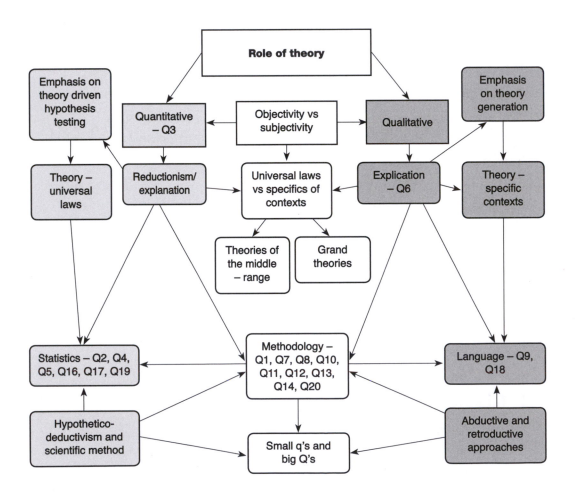

Chapter 3
The basics of experimental design

This chapter covers topics such as why experiments are used in psychology, basic independent samples designs, basic repeated measures designs, the strengths and weaknesses of the experimental method, common analysis techniques and their associated considerations.

Select one of the possible answers for each question.

Foundation level questions

1. Complete the following statement: In an experiment, we manipulate a _____ variable, whilst _____ all other variables and measuring change in a _____ variable.

    A. Independent, observing, dependent.

    B. Dependent, observing, independent.

    C. Independent, controlling, dependent.

    D. Dependent, controlling, independent.

    Your answer: [ ] C ✓

2. What are the key reasons for conducting experiments?

    A. Experiments have the greatest convergent validity of all research methods.

    B. The experimental method is the best available research method for establishing causal relationships. ✓

    C. Experiments are the best descriptive research method available. ✗

    D. All of the above.

    Your answer: [ ] B ✓

3. When an experiment fulfils the three conditions for <u>causal inference</u>: covariation, time-order relationship and elimination of plausible alternative causes, it is said to have what?

   A. Convergent validity.

   B. Discriminant validity.

   C. External validity.

   D. Internal validity.

   Your answer: D (cheated) ✓

   Types of validity

4. The degree to which an experimental environment mimics real life is known as what?

   A. Critical realism.

   B. Experimental realism.

   C. Mundane realism.

   D. None of the above.

   Your answer: C (checked) ✓

5. What is the method of controlling for confounding variables in research, through disguising the aims of the research to participants but not the experimenter?

   A. Using standardised instructions.

   B. Double-blind technique.

   C. Randomisation of participants in conditions.

   D. Single-blind technique.

   Your answer: A ✗D

6. If a non-probability sample or non-random sampling method is used, there are potential implications for what?

   A. The type of statistical test that can be used to analyse the data.

   B. Sampling error.

   C. The generalisability of research findings.

   D. All of the above.

   Your answer: D ✓

   Sampling methods

7. Counterbalancing is an example of a method of dealing with what?

   A. Order effects.

   B. Unequal sample sizes.

   C. Unrepresentative groups.

   D. None of the above.

Your answer: ☒ A ✓

8. Which of the following terms refers to a technique which is applied to groups of participants to control for a confounding variable?

   A. Random assessment.

   B. Random assignment.

   C. Random examination.

   D. Random evaluation.

Your answer: ☒ B ✓

9. There are two ways in which participants can fail to complete an experiment which are referred to as what?   *: compl. crashing/wrong instructions read out*

   A. Mechanical and selective.   *subject loss threatens internal validity*

   B. Automatic and selective.

   C. Mechanical and systemic.   *How to fail a task*

   D. Automatic and systemic.

Your answer: ☒ B × A

10. In experimental research, statistics which are used to determine whether an independent variable has a reliable effect on a dependent variable are known as what?

   A. Inferential.

   B. Descriptive.

   C. Evaluative.

   D. Hypothetical.

Your answer: ☒ A ✓

11. Practice effects are particularly problematic for which type of research design?

   A. Survey research.

   B. Independent samples design.

   C. Repeated-measures design.

   D. All of the above.

Your answer: ☒ .C ✓

Advanced level questions

12. The following are characteristics associated with what type of research design? No order effects, variation between individuals in different groups may confound results, less economical on number of participants required.

   A. Independent samples.

   B. Repeated measures.✗

   C. Matched pairs.

   D. Case studies.

Your answer: ☒ A̶ C ✗ A

13. What are the four assumptions which underpin parametric statistical tests?

   A̶. Representative samples, independence of observations, homogeneity of variance and data must at least be measured at interval level.

   B. Normally distributed data, independence of observations, homogeneity of variance and data must at least be measured at interval level.

   C. Representative samples, normally distributed data, independence of observations and data must at least be measured at ordinal level.

   D. Normally distributed data, independence of observations, independent variables must not be correlated and data must at least be measured at ordinal level.

Your answer: ☒ D ✗ B

14. In relation to assessing statistical significance, which of these statements is correct regarding the null hypothesis?

    A. A null hypothesis states that there is no relationship between the variables of interest in the population from which the sample was drawn.

    B. A null hypothesis states that there is no relationship between the variables of interest in the sample.

    C. A null hypothesis states that there is a relationship between the variables of interest in the population from which the sample was drawn.

    D. A null hypothesis states that there is a relationship between the variables of interest in the sample.

Your answer: [ ] A ✓

15. Which of the following measures the strength of the relationship between the independent and dependent variables in an experiment?

    A. Coefficient of determination.

    B. Confidence intervals.

    C. Effect size.

    D. Significance value.

Your answer: [ ] D × C

16. Which of the following is true regarding the relationship between effect sizes and sample sizes?

    A. Effect sizes are independent of sample sizes.

    B. Effect sizes are bigger when sample sizes are larger. ×

    C. Effect sizes are bigger when sample sizes are smaller. ×

    D. Effect sizes are more likely to be significant with smaller sample sizes. ×

Your answer: [ ] A ✓

17. Complete the following paragraph using one of the options below.
Repeated measures designs (also known as _____ designs) are often used when researchers need to conduct and experiment when _____ participants are available, or to study changes in participants' behaviour _____. In repeated measures designs, participants serve as their _____.

A. Between-subjects, few, over time, own controls.

B. Within-subjects, few, over time, own controls.

C. Within-subjects, many, again, own controls.

D. Between-subjects, many, again, own evaluators.

Your answer: B ✓

18. Complete the following sentence:
A statistically significant outcome is one that has what?

A. A small likelihood of occurring if the null hypothesis were true.

B. A large likelihood of occurring if the null hypothesis were true.

C. A small likelihood of occurring if the alternative hypothesis were true.

D. A large likelihood of occurring if the alternative hypothesis were true.

Your answer: A ✓

19. If you compare the 95% confidence intervals for two different groups' means and they do not overlap, what does this suggest?

A. We can be confident that the sample means for the two groups differ.

B. We cannot be confident that the population means for the two groups are different.

C. We can be confident that the population means for the two groups differ.

D. We cannot make any conclusions about whether the two groups' population means are different or not.

Your answer: A ✗

20. Which of the following options are the two most commonly used descriptive statistics to summarise the results of experiments?

A. Mean and standard error.

B. Mean and percentages.

C. Mean and standard deviation. ✓

D. Mean and percentiles.

Your answer: ⬚   C ✓

21. Why might a repeated-measures design be more sensitive and involve less error variation than a between-groups design?

A. There will be less variability between the same individuals' scores over the time of an experiment in a repeated measures design, than there would be between different participants in a random group design. ✓

B. You can exert greater control in a repeated-measures design than in a between-groups design.

C. Practice effects mean that participants get better at the tasks they have to complete in the research so there is less error. ✓

D. All of the above.

Your answer: ⬚   C ✗A

22. Which of the following are characteristics of natural-groups experimental designs?

A. Individual-difference variables (subject variables) are selected rather than manipulated to form groups.

B. Natural-groups designs represent a form of correlation research in which covariations between natural-groups variables and dependent variables are explored.

C. Causal inferences cannot be made regarding the effects of natural-groups variables because it is not possible to rule out alternative explanations for group differences.

D. All of the above.

Your answer: ⬚ D ✓

63·63%.

Extended multiple-choice question

Complete the following paragraph using the items listed below. Not all of the items will be consistent with the paragraph and not all items can be used. Items can be used only once.

There are two types of _____ [H] _____ design, the complete and the incomplete design, which require different techniques to control for _____ [A] _____, which are broadly referred to as _____ techniques. A _____ [J] _____ design involves ensuring that practice effects are balanced for each participant by administering the conditions to each participant several times using _____ orders each time. In an _____ design, however, each condition is administered to each participant _____, and the order of administering the conditions is varied across participants rather than for each participant.

Optional items

A. practice effects

B. twice

C. the same

D. extraneous variables

E. incomplete

F. only once

G. between-groups

H. repeated-measures

I. counterbalancing

J. complete

K. different

L. same order

Essay questions for Chapter 3

Once you have completed the MCQs above you are ready to tackle some essay questions. You might like to select three or four topics and make notes on them. One way of doing this is to create a concept map. The first question has been done for you and you can see how the knowledge required links to some of the MCQs in this chapter.

1. What are the strengths and weaknesses of experimental research? Discuss, providing examples of research to illustrate your answer.

2. Critically discuss the purposes served by descriptive and inferential statistics, and evaluate their strengths and weaknesses using examples of relevant research to support your argument.

3. Describe and evaluate the difficulties in designing a research study to assess causal relationships between variables, and discuss how they can be overcome, providing evidence to support your conclusions.

4. Can true experiments ever be conducted in psychological research? Critically discuss this debate, providing relevant examples to highlight the key issues.

5. Compare the independent-samples and repeated-measures designs to research. What are their strengths and weaknesses and how might an experiment be designed to overcome them? Provide evidence to support your arguments.

6. Compare and evaluate the experimental method with the survey method for investigating the hypothesis that playing violent video games leads to aggressive behaviour.

7. Compare the true experimental method and quasi-experimental methods. Critically evaluate these two different approaches' strengths and weaknesses, providing evidence to support your conclusions.

8. Critically evaluate the strategies available to psychological researchers to avoid confounding variables in experimental research.

Chapter 3 essay question 1: concept map

What are the strengths and weaknesses of experimental research? Discuss, providing examples of research to illustrate your answer.

The concept map opposite provides an example of how the first sample essay may be conceptualised. Examining what experimental research entails, the considerations underpinning it (e.g. hypothetico-deductivism), and the critiques offered by critical social psychological approaches (e.g. social constructionism) is necessary before conclusions on this issue can be drawn. Exploring alternative methodologies proposed by researchers working from different paradigms will help to understand more fully the difficulties in conducting research and the appeal of the experimental method.

Remember that it is important to link your answers to other topic areas not covered in this chapter.

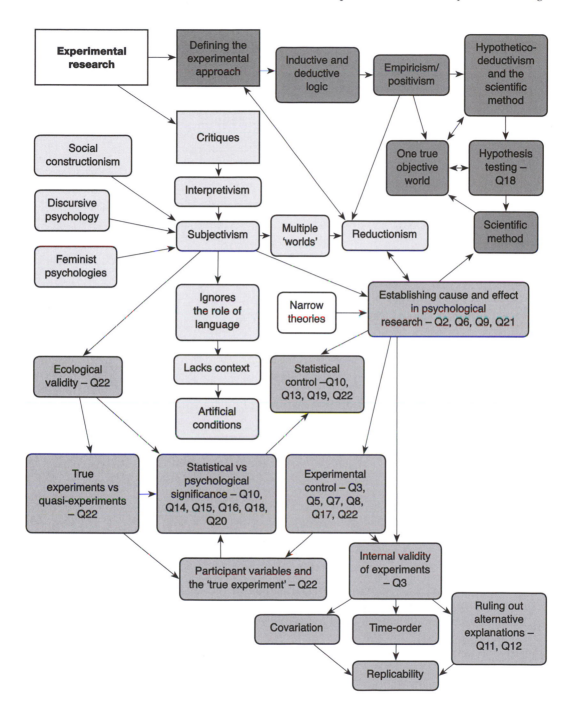

Chapter 4
Designing complex experiments

This chapter will include questions on complex experimental designs, including research involving more than two independent variables, mixed design studies, the strengths and weaknesses of complex experiments, statistical analysis techniques used with complex experimental designs and their associated considerations.

Select one of the possible answers for each question.

Foundation level questions

1. What is a 'complex design' in psychological research?

    A. Research involving extremely large samples.

    B. Research which seeks to study the effects of two or more independent variables in one experiment.

    C. Research which uses many different statistical procedures to analyse the results.

    D. All of the above.

    Your answer: ☒ D X B

2. What is a <u>Latin square</u>? x

    A. A counterbalancing technique used to eliminate practice and order effects.

    B. A mathematical formula used to calculate the number of conditions needed for an experiment.

    C. A mathematical formula used to calculate the sample size required by an experiment in order to detect the desired effect size.

    D. A method of calculating significance in complex research designs.

    Your answer: ☒ D X A

3. What is meant by a 2 × 2 design?

A. A research design with two independent variables, each with two levels.

B. A research design with two groups, with two participants in each group.

C. A research design with two independent variables and two dependent variables.

D. A research design with two groups of participants, each with two conditions.

Your answer: A ✓

4. In a 2 × 2 × 4 research design, how many conditions will there be?

A. 3.

B. (8.)   8×2

C. 12.

D. 16.

Your answer: B × D

5. What does the term 'mixed design' refer to?

A. A research design which incorporates two or more questionnaires. ✗

B. A research design which incorporates both descriptive and inferential statistics. ✗

C. A research design which incorporates both an independent-groups variable and a repeated-measures variable. ✓

D. All of the above. ✗

Your answer: C ✓

6. The overall effect of each independent variable in a complex design is called what?

A. A main effect.

B. An interaction effect.

C. A moderator.

D. A mediator.

Your answer: A ✓

7. In a research report, a design is described as 'two-way unrelated samples'. What does this suggest?

   A. There are two independent variables and both are repeated measures in nature (e.g. differences within groups are studied).

   B. There are two independent variables and both use independent samples (e.g. differences between groups are studied).

   C. There are two dependent variables and both use independent samples (e.g. differences between groups are studied).

   D. There are two dependent variables and both are repeated measures in nature (e.g. differences within groups are studied).

Your answer: ☒ B ✓

8. What is a factorial design?

   A. A design with more than one independent variable in which the levels of the one independent variable are varied across all the levels of the other independent variable(s).

   B. A design with more than one independent variable in which a selection of all possible combinations of the levels of the one variable are varied across all the levels of the other independent variable(s).

   C. A design with more than one dependent variable in which a selection of all possible combinations of the levels of the one dependent variable are explored in relation to all the levels of the other dependent variable(s).

   D. All of the above.

Your answer: ☒ A ✓

9. A research study involves looking at the impact of two different interventions on university students' stress levels. Participants are randomly assigned either to a stress-inoculation intervention or a meditation-based intervention. They are asked to complete a perceived stress questionnaire prior to the intervention, at two weeks, four weeks and eight weeks during the intervention. Although the research started with 80 participants, by the eight week assessment only 47 participants still remained. Choose from the list of options the statement which applies most accurately to this scenario.

   A. Random allocation of students to the two intervention groups strengthens this design.

   B. Without a control group it is difficult to establish whether changes to participants' levels of stress were effected solely by the interventions. ✓

   C. The large drop-out rate in the research is a cause for concern as the remaining sample may no longer be representative. ✓

   D. All of the above.

Your answer:  D ✓

10. The 'differential transfer' refers to what?

   A. When a participant's performance in a research study is affected by the performance of other participants in their group.

   B. When a participant's performance is affected by participant variables, such as age.

   C. When performance in one condition in a research design differs depending on the condition preceding it.

   D. When participants' performance is affected by differing degrees of commitment to the task they are asked to complete.

Your answer: D ✗

Advanced level questions

11. In the statistical analysis of a complex design, what do the means for a main effect represent?

   A. The overall performance/score at each level of a particular independent, variable, collapsed across (averaged over) the levels of the other independent variable.

   B. The overall performance/score at each level of a particular independent variable at each level of the other independent variable.

   C. The overall performance/score at each level of a particular independent variable, collapsed across (averaged over) the levels of the dependent variable.

   D. None of the above.

Your answer: [ ]    B xA

12. If a statistically significant interaction effect is identified in the analysis of a complex design, the source of the interaction effect can be identified by examining the effect of one independent variable at one level of the other independent variable. What is this effect known as?

   A. A simple main effect.

   B. A simple interaction effect.

   C. A complex main effect.

   D. A complex interaction effect.

Your answer: [ ] BA ✓

13. If no interaction effect occurs in a complex design and the effects of each independent variable can be generalised across the levels of the other independent variable, what implications does this have for the external validity of the independent variables?

   A. It remains the same.

   B. It increases.

   C. It decreases.

   D. It is not possible to say what implications this has for the external validity of the independent variables.

Your answer: [ ]    C xB

14. Complete the following paragraph using the options below.

According to <u>Underwood and Shaughnessy</u> (1975), complex designs may be used to make causal inferences based on _____ design research. Firstly, _____ must be developed explaining why a difference should occur in the performance of groups that have been differentiated on the bases of an individual-difference variable. Secondly, a relevant variable to _____ must be identified, which is presumed to influence the likelihood that this theoretical process will occur. Thirdly, the researcher must test for an _____ effect between the manipulated variable and the individual-differences variable.

A. Natural groups, an idea, manipulate, interaction.

B. Natural groups, a theory, observe, main.

C. Random groups, a theory, manipulate, interaction.

D. Natural groups, a theory, manipulate, interaction.

Your answer: ▨ C ×D

15. A study seeks to explore the relationship between increasing amounts of practice on performance during a physical fitness test by comparing participants who were given either 10, 30 or 60 minutes to practise, doing either hard or easy exercises. The dependent variable is the percentage of exercises that each participant was able to complete in a 15-minute test period. How can this study avoid a 'ceiling effect'?

A. Ensure a dependent variable will not artificially impose a restriction on the amount of exercise possible by testing participants with a greater number of exercises than anyone could be expected to complete in the time allotted for the test. ✓

B. Only select participants who are unlikely to be able to complete the maximum number of exercises possible in the allotted time. × bias

C. If participants reach the maximum number of exercises possible in the allotted time, this is OK – it just means that they are very good at exercising. ✓ boo

D. If participants reach the maximum number of exercises possible in the allotted time, they should automatically be put into the easy exercise group because they found the exercise tasks easy. No bias

Your answer: ▨ A ✓

16. In a complex research design with three independent variables, what does a three-way interaction effect represent?

A. A three-way interaction effect occurs when the interaction of two of the independent variables differs depending on the level of a third independent variable.

B. A three-way interaction effect occurs when two of the independent variables differ, regardless of the level of the third independent variable.

C. A three-way interaction effect occurs when one of the three independent variables differs depending on the level of one of the other independent variables.

D. None of the above.

Your answer: ☒   A ✓

17. What is the name of the statistical procedure commonly used which allows for the statistical control of a variable which was either improperly controlled (or could not be controlled through research design), which may have a confounding effect on the relationship between an independent variable(s) and a dependent variable?

A. Kruskal-Wallis test.

B. Analysis of covariance (ANCOVA).

C. Chi-square goodness-of-fit test.

D. Mann-Whitney U test.

Your answer: ☒   B ✓

18. When running post-hoc analyses (multiple comparisons), there is an increase in which type of error?

A. Familywise error (the risk of making a type I error).

B. Total error (the risk of making a type II error).

C. Participant error (the risk of making a type I error).

D. Empirical error (the risk of making a type II error).

Your answer: ☒   A ✓

19. Why are complex designs used in psychological research?

A. Psychological theories often predict that two or more independent variables interact to influence behaviour. Complex designs are able to test such theories.

B. Research into theories can sometimes produce contradictory findings – studying interaction effects in complex designs can be instrumental in resolving these contradictions.

C. Researchers can use complex designs to make causal inferences about natural-groups variables when they test a theory for why natural groups may differ.

D. All of the above.

Your answer: D ✓

20. If the results of a 2×2 design are summarised in a table, what method can be used to assess the presence or absence of an interaction effect?

A. The addition method.

B. The subtraction method.

C. The division method.

D. The multiplication method.

Your answer:

Extended multiple-choice question

Research using a complex design is conducted to explore the effect of an intervention aimed at reducing stress for primary and secondary school teachers. Prior to the intervention and immediately after the intervention, teachers completed a self-report measure of perceived stress. The graph below represents the results of the data analysis. From the following list of options, what conclusions could be appropriately drawn from examining this graph alone?

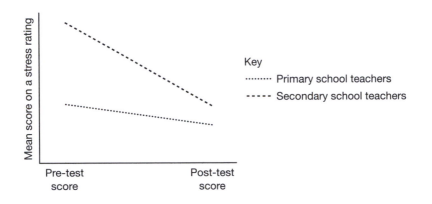

Optional items

A. There appears to be an interaction effect between school type and the intervention: secondary school teachers' stress scores appear to have decreased to a greater extent than primary school teachers' stress scores.

B. There appears to be an interaction effect between school type and the intervention: primary school teachers' stress scores appear to have decreased to a greater extent than secondary school teachers' stress scores.

C. This experiment should be described as a repeated-measures design.

D. From examining this graph, there does not appear to be any evidence for an interaction effect in the data.

E. It is not possible to say whether any differences between pre-test and post-test scores are statistically significant from examining this graph alone.

F. This experiment should be described as a mixed design.

G. There appears to be a statistically significant difference between the pre-test and post-test scores for both primary and secondary teachers.

H. An interaction effect is evidenced by the fact that primary school teachers score lower on the measure of stress than the secondary school teachers at both the pre- and post-test.

I. This experiment should be described as a between-groups design.

J. There appears to be a statistically significant difference between the pre-test and post-test scores for secondary school teachers only.

K. The graph provides evidence that systematic error is present in the research design.

Essay questions for Chapter 4

Once you have completed the MCQs above you are ready to tackle some essay questions. You might like to select three or four topics and make notes on them. One way of doing this is to create a concept map. The first question has been done for you and you can see how the knowledge required links to some of the MCQs in this chapter.

1. Describe and evaluate the situations in which a psychological researcher may be required to use a complex design.

2. Critically describe and evaluate the strengths and weaknesses of the mixed design.

3. Critically discuss what interaction effects are, how they can be identified in research and what they can tell us. Provide examples from psychological research to illustrate your answer.

4. Describe and evaluate statistical control and experimental control techniques in complex research designs.

5. Discuss the issues involved in using naturally occurring groups in complex research designs. Provide examples from psychological research to illustrate your answer.

6. You are asked by a hospital to design a research study exploring the effectiveness of a social support group for men and women who are undergoing treatment for cancer. How would you design a research study to explore the effectiveness of the support group overall and also examine whether there are gender differences?

7. Describe and evaluate the possible threats to the validity of a complex research design?

8. Describe and discuss mediated, moderated and suppressed relationships between variables. How can they be identified using statistical techniques?

Chapter 4 essay question 1: concept map

Describe and evaluate the situations in which a psychological researcher may be required to use a complex research design.

The concept map below provides an example of how the first sample essay may be conceptualised. Examination of what a complex research design actually is leads to several subtopics. Exploring these subtopics will allow the strengths and limitations of complex research designs, and the situations when it is appropriate to use them, to be assessed. A good answer to this question will also provide an insight into the difficulties which these research designs must overcome in order to be effective (e.g. experimental and statistical control).

Remember that it is important to link your answers to other topic areas not covered in this chapter.

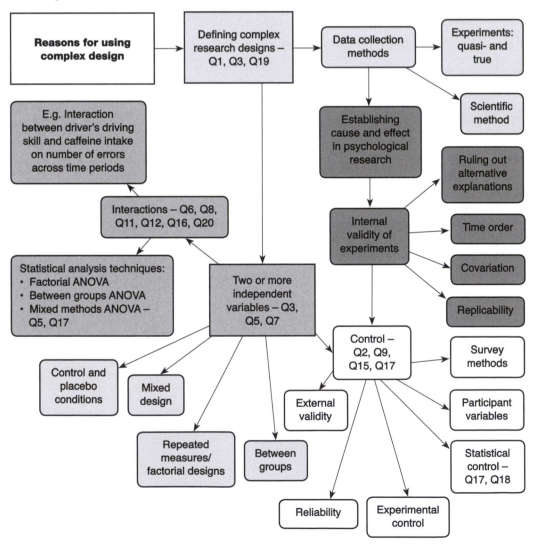

Chapter 5
Case studies, single-case and small-n designs

This chapter will cover the case study method, single-participant experimental designs, small-n designs, their characteristics and applications, common methods of analysis used with these research designs, and the strengths and weaknesses of these approaches to research.

Select one of the possible answers for each question.

Foundation level questions

1. What was Bromley (1986, p8) describing with the statement 'natural occurrences with definable boundaries'?

   A. A unit.

   B. An event.   *Bromley (1986)*

   C. A case.

   D. A phenomenon.

   Your answer: ☑ D ✗ C

2. Which of the following statements is true regarding the case study method?

   A. Case studies can use both qualitative and quantitative methodology.

   B. Case studies are particularly useful if conducting research with participants with rare conditions.

   C. Case studies have been used in psychology to form the basis of generalised theoretical principles.

   D. All of the above.

   Your answer: B ✗ D

3. Which of the following features is commonly associated with the case study method?

   A. Idiographic perspective.

   B. Attention to contextual data.

   C. Triangulation.

   D. All of the above.

Your answer: D ✓

4. Which methodology used in case study research did Gordon (1968) propose?

   A. Twenty statements test.

   B. Repertory grids.

   C. Triangulation.

   D. All of the above.

Your answer: D ✗ A

5. What was Silverman (1993) describing, when he referred to 'respondent validation'?

   A. Where a researcher provides positive feedback to a respondent to encourage them in their participation in the research.

   B. Where the participant has a positive experience during the participation in research which leads to an increase in self-esteem.

   C. Where a researcher presents their emerging interpretation to the participant to obtain feedback.

   D. None of the above.

Your answer: C ✓

6. In which approach do small-n designs (also known as single-participant experimental designs) have their roots?

   A. The study of behaviour developed by Skinner.

   B. The study of dreams developed by Freud.

   C. The study of structuralism developed by Wundt.

   D. The study of the 'stream of consciousness' developed by James.

Your answer: A B ✗

7. According to Shaughnessy, Zechmeister and Zechmeister (2009), small-n designs form part of an approach known as what?

   A. Experimental analysis of events.

   B. Experimental analysis of behaviour.

   C. Experimental analysis of reactions.

   D. Experimental analysis of physiological psychology.

   Your answer: B ✓

8. In small-n designs, experimental control is often demonstrated through what?

   A. Systematically manipulating an independent variable across experimental conditions.

   B. Using multiple methods of inferential statistical analysis to explore whether statistically significant results are reliable.

   C. Using multiple methods of data collection to explore the validity of the relationship between the variables.

   D. Using extremely specific research questions and hypotheses to ensure data collection is focused on the specific issue of interest.

   Your answer: C ✗

9. Which of the following is a frequent criticism of single-participant research designs?

   A. External validity.

   B. Internal validity.

   C. Both A and B.

   D. None of the above.

   Your answer: C ✗

10. What are the advantages of using archival data in case studies and small-n designs?

    A. They are unobtrusive measures which are a valuable alternative to direct observation.

    B. They can be used to test the external validity of laboratory findings.

    C. They can be used for triangulation purposes.

    D. All of the above.

    Your answer: D ✓

Advanced level questions

11. Complete the following paragraph, using the options below.

Case studies which are chosen because they are interesting in their own right are referred to as _____, whereas case studies which constitute exemplars of a more general phenomenon are known as _____ case studies. _____ case studies tend to be utilised in the former, whereas _____ case studies allow a researcher the opportunity to generate and refine new theories.

    A. Intrinsic, instrumental, single, multiple.

    B. Instrumental, intrinsic, single, multiple.

    C. Intrinsic, instrumental, multiple, single.

    D. Instrumental, intrinsic, single, multiple.

Your answer: [ ]

12. Case studies which are not explored in terms of existing theoretical formulations but still hope to generate new insights into (and a better understanding of) a phenomenon are called what?

    A. Explanatory case studies.

    B. Descriptive case studies.

    C. Explicative case studies.

    D. Circumstantial case studies.

Your answer: [ ]

13. Hamel (1993) argues that researchers need to make a distinction between what?

    A. The 'object of study' and 'the case'.

    B. 'Qualitative' and 'quantitative' case studies.

    C. Case studies using an individual as the case ('individual' case studies) and case studies using an event as the case ('event' case studies).

    D. All of the above.

Your answer: [ ]

14. Which of the following is an example of a methodology not suited to case study research?

   A. Semi-structured interviews.

   B. Diary methods.

   C. Focus groups.

   D. None of the above.

Your answer:

15. Which of the following responses describes key ethical issues involved in case study research?

   A. The interactive nature of the research may 'change' the respondent.

   B. Case studies often involve a large degree of deception.

   C. They can be intrusive and invasive.

   D. Both A and C.

Your answer:

16. What is the key characteristic which differentiates case study research from small-n experimental design research?

   A. Case studies lack the degree of control found in small-n experimental designs.

   B. Case studies tend to explore events, whereas small-n designs tend to explore individuals.

   C. Both A and B.

   D. None of the above.

Your answer:

17. A psychologist carrying out case study research uses multiple sources of data (such as interviews and official documents) to investigate the same phenomenon. What is this an example of?

   A. Triangulation.

   B. Cyclical research.

   C. Baseline measurement.

   D. None of the above.

Your answer:

18. In single-participant experimental designs, little emphasis is often placed on what?

    A. Defining behaviour.

    B. Observing behaviour.

    C. Recording behaviour.

    D. Inferential statistical analysis of behaviour.

Your answer:

19. Which of the following are common experimental designs in single-case and small-n experimental research designs?

    A. ABAB design.

    B. Multiple baseline design across individuals.

    C. Multiple baseline design across behaviours.

    D. All of the above.

Your answer:

20. In single case research using the multiple baseline design, how many baselines do Hersen and Barlow (1976) recommend as being adequate?

    A. 1–2.

    B. 2–3.

    C. 3–4.

    D. 4–5.

Your answer:

Extended multiple-choice question

Complete the following paragraphs using the items listed below. Not all of the items will be consistent with the paragraph and not all items can be used. Items can be used only once.

Case studies have a number of advantages. Case studies can provide a chance to study _____ phenomena, such as patients with prosopagnosia (a disorder of face perception), which it would not be possible to study otherwise. Case studies can be used to _____ theory, for example when the behaviour of a single case contradicts theoretical principles or claims. Alternatively, this type of research can be used to _____ a theory, although it should never be taken as conclusive. Finally, case studies are idiographic in nature but can be used to complement _____ research, for example in clinical research.

It should also be recognised that the case study method has disadvantages too: the main criticism concerns the inability to make _____, because _____ variables are not controlled. Also, there is a high risk of _____ or bias in data collection, which may lead to misleading interpretations of the findings from such research. Lastly, there is also an issue regarding the degree to which research findings can be _____.

Optional items

A. rare

B. observer bias

C. hermeneutic

D. challenge

E. extraneous

F. common

G. causal inferences

H. inter-rater reliability

I. generalised

J. tentatively support

K. nomothetic

L. quantified

Essay questions for Chapter 5

Once you have completed the MCQs above you are ready to tackle some essay questions. You might like to select three or four topics and make notes on them. One way of doing this is to create a concept map. The first question has been done for you and you can see how the knowledge required links to some of the MCQs in this chapter.

1. Discuss the issues surrounding the generalisability of research findings from case study, single-case and small-n design research.

2. Discuss the potential applications of case study research and small-n design research in applied research. What are the potential limitations in such research?

3. Critically discuss the role of theory in case study research, providing examples of relevant research to illustrate your answer.

4. Compare and evaluate the single-participant design with the multiple-group design.

5. Allport was a staunch advocate of the case study approach to research, suggesting that nomothetic research was inadequate for understanding human behaviour. Critically evaluate this position, providing examples from research to illustrate your answer.

6. Some psychologists argue that case studies, or single-participant designs, have no place in scientific research. Critically discuss this position, providing examples of theory and research to support your arguments.

7. Critically examine the role of official documents and archival data in case study research. What are the strengths and weaknesses of using these sources of data?

8. Critically discuss the ethical considerations involved in case study research and how they can be mitigated.

Chapter 5 essay question 1: concept map

Discuss the issues surrounding the generalisability of research findings from case study, single-case and small-n design studies.

The concept map below provides an example of how the first sample essay may be conceptualised. Examining the different ways in which "generalisability" is conceptualised in case study, single-case and small-n research designs, and how this differs depending on whether a quantitative or qualitative approach is adopted, reveals several subtopics. Exploring these issues provides insight into the different methods of establishing generalisability and the degree of emphasis placed upon this by different research approaches. It also highlights the difficulties faced by researchers in demonstrating generalisability (e.g. applying their findings to other situations or groups) and how these issues can be managed or overcome.

Remember that it is important to link your answers to other topic areas not covered in this chapter.

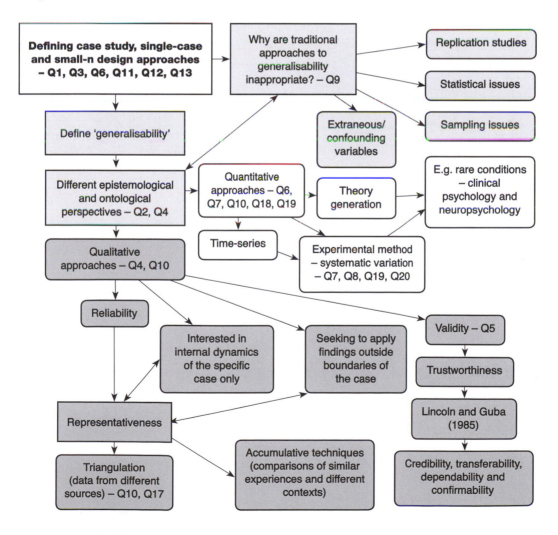

Chapter 6
Observational methods

This chapter covers the main observational methods used in psychological research, including diary methods, controlled and naturalistic observation, covert and naturalistic observation, participant and non-participant observation, and their associated strengths and weaknesses.

Select one of the possible answers for each question.

Foundation level questions

1. Who suggested that the five features that can be used to distinguish between different types of observation were: degree of researcher participation; degree of researcher reflexivity; extent to which the observation is covert; extent to which it is standardised; and whether or not it takes place in a natural setting?

   A. Jonathan Potter.

   B. Carla Willig.

   C. Uwe Flick.

   D. Michel Foucault.

   Your answer: ☐

2. Which of the following is the least commonly used observational method in psychological research?

   A. Participant observation.

   B. Non-participant observation.

   C. Diary method.

   D. These methods are all used equally often in research.

   Your answer: ☐

3. Which of the following is *not* one of the three broad categories of research notes written in observational research?

   A. Substantive notes.

   B. Methodological notes.

   C. Analytical notes.

   D. Evaluative notes.

Your answer:

4. Diary methods are not commonly used in psychological research for what reason?

   A. Place a considerable burden on participants.

   B. Can be very unreliable (e.g. people forget to fill them in).

   C. May affect the participant's behaviour, leading to a misrepresentation of their behaviour.

   D. All of the above.

Your answer:

5. Structured observation is also known as what?

   A. Systematic observation.

   B. Engineered observation.

   C. Organised observation.

   D. Controlled observation.

Your answer:

6. Webb, Campbell, Schwartz and Sechrest (1966) make a distinction between which two types of non-participant research?

   A. Honest and contrived.

   B. Open and closed.

   C. Simple and contrived.

   D. Simple and complex.

Your answer:

7. Why are observational methods used?

    A. Research has consistently identified a gap between stated and actual behaviour.

    B. They are purely qualitative and so afford a better understanding of human interaction.

    C. Experimental approaches to research into social interactions may lack ecological validity.

    D. Both A and C.

Your answer:

8. What term is given to the categories of behaviour that are to be observed and information on how this behaviour should be allocated to categories?

    A. Observation schedule and reference list.

    B. Reference list and coding scheme.

    C. Observation scheme and coding schedule.

    D. Observation schedule and coding scheme.

Your answer:

9. What type of sampling procedure involves briefly observing an entire group of individuals at regular intervals and recording their behaviour at that specific moment in time?

    A. Focal sampling.

    B. Scan sampling.

    C. Ad libitum sampling.

    D. Behaviour sampling.

Your answer:

10. What is the name of the effect which can confound a researcher's data, whereby participants become aware that they are being observed and alter their behaviour?

    A. Social effect.

    B. Reactive effect.

    C. Negative effect.

    D. All of these are examples of this effect.

Your answer:

Advanced level questions

11. A psychologist is designing an observational research study. She is planning to observe people in department stores to understand consumer behaviour. The department store has given her permission to sit unobtrusively and observe people in both the men's and women's wear sections. The researcher has designed extremely detailed and specific rules for the observation and recording of the behaviour, including both verbal and non-verbal behaviour. What type of observation is this an example of?

   A. Simple, structured, participant observation.

   B. Contrived, unstructured, participant observation.

   C. Simple, structured, non-participant observation.

   D. Contrived, unstructured, non-participant observation.

Your answer:

12. Which of the following is an undesirable characteristic of an observation schedule?

   A. Large numbers of types of behaviour required to ensure everything about the interaction is recorded.

   B. Detailed and specific instructions on how to allocate behaviour to different categories.

   C. Mutually exclusive behaviour categories to ensure the coding scheme is unambiguous.

   D. Allowing a separate category for unexpected behaviour which has not been pre-coded but is very pertinent to the research.

Your answer:

13. Which of the following is a well-known method of observing and recording behaviour in research?

   A. Incidents.

   B. Periods of time.

   C. Time sampling.

   D. All of the above.

Your answer:

14. Which of the following is an issue encountered by researchers when conducting structured observational research?

A. Probability sampling of participants.

B. Random selection of time period.

C. Random selection of environments (e.g. schools, shopping centres).

D. All of the above.

Your answer:

15. A study conducted by Larson et al. (1996) into adolescent interactions with their families involved giving participants electronic pagers and asking them to report on their behaviour when randomly 'beeped'. What is this an example of?

A. Narrative record.

B. The experience sampling method (ESM).

C. Field simulation.

D. None of the above.

Your answer:

16. Webb, Campbell, Schwartz and Sechrest (1966) suggested that role selection, the guinea-pig effect, response set and content-irrelevant methods variance are the four components which comprise what?

A. The reactive effect.

B. The Hawthorne effect.

C. The social desirability effect.

D. The social facilitation effect.

Your answer:

17. What is the name given by Salancik (1979) to an observational study in which the researcher directly intervenes in or manipulates a natural setting so they can observe what happens as a result of this intervention?

A. Field simulation.

B. Quasi-experiment.

C. Field study.

D. Structured participant observation.

Your answer:

18. What form of observational method did Jane Goodall most frequently adopt in her research into the behaviour of chimpanzees?

    A. Participant observation.

    B. Naturalistic observation.

    C. Indirect observation.

    D. None of the above.

    Your answer:

19. What form of qualitative observational method (which often uses video recordings of behaviour) aims to provide a faithful reproduction of behaviour as it actually occurrs?

    A. Illustrative record.

    B. Exemplary record.

    C. Narrative record.

    D. Explicative record.

    Your answer:

20. Which of the following levels of measurement are possible in observational research?

    A. Nominal.

    B. Ordinal.

    C. Ratio.

    D. All of the above.

    Your answer:

Extended multiple-choice question

Please complete the following paragraph using the items listed below. Not all of the items will be consistent with the paragraph and not all items can be used. Items can be used only once.

Observational research can be both _____ and _____ in nature. It is often used in research to overcome the issue of the gap between _____ behaviour and _____ behaviour and is believed by some researchers to provide a more _____ and _____ picture of human behaviour than survey and interview methods. However, it faces a number of criticisms; there is a risk of imposing a potentially _____, in the form of a _____, on the behaviour to be observed. However, this could be overcome by running _____ research using _____ observation to ensure the coding scheme is relevant. Also, some researchers argue that by observing only overt behaviour these methods are unable to capture _____ and _____. Linked to this is the concern that observational research loses sight of the _____ in which the behaviour occurs and can generate scraps of fragmented information. The difficulty then faced by the researcher is to organise this information in a coherent, accurate and meaningful way.

Optional items

A. irrelevant framework

B. quantitative

C. valid

D. coding scheme

E. intention

F. accurate

G. meaning

H. pilot

I. qualitative

J. actual

K. stated

L. context

M. unstructured

Essay questions for Chapter 6

Once you have completed the MCQs above you are ready to tackle some essay questions. You might like to select three or four topics and make notes on them. One way of doing this is to create a concept map. The first question has been done for you and you can see how the knowledge required links to some of the MCQs in this chapter.

1. Describe and evaluate the different strategies available to researchers for observing human behaviour.

2. Critically discuss the suggestion that structured observations provide more reliable, precise and accurate information about events than interviews or questionnaires.

3. Compare and evaluate quantitative and qualitative approaches to observational research. What are the different goals of these two different approaches to research?

4. What are the ethical considerations in observational research? Critically examine participant, non-participant and field simulation approaches in your answer.

5. Describe and evaluate the different sampling issues which psychological researchers face when designing observational research studies.

6. Critically examine the ethical issues involved in participant and covert observational studies. How can these issues be overcome or mitigated?

7. Compare the field simulation and structured observational approaches to investigating the effect of interruption on students' revision behaviour in university libraries. Critically evaluate the issues these two different approaches might face in studying this phenomenon.

8. Compare and evaluate participant, controlled and naturalistic observational research approaches. Provide examples of relevant research to illustrate their strengths and weaknesses, and the ethical issues they both raise.

Chapter 6 essay question 1: concept map

Describe and evaluate the different strategies available to researchers for observing human behaviour.

The concept map opposite provides an example of how the first sample essay may be conceptualised. Consideration of the different types of observation and coding schedules leads to several subtopics, which must be critically evaluated before conclusions can be drawn. In this case the evidence suggests that different types of observation are associated with different methodological and ethical issues, which have an impact on researchers' decisions when choosing the most appropriate methodology to use. Exploring the different strategies adopted by researchers to eliminate or mitigate these issues will provide a full answer to the question posed.

Remember that it is important to link your answers to other topic areas not covered in this chapter.

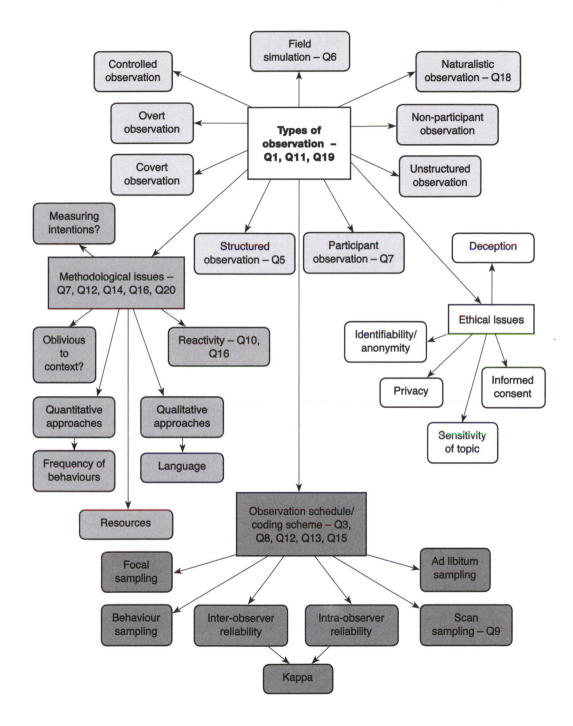

Chapter 7
Survey research

This chapter covers topics such as questionnaire construction, sampling methods common to survey research, commonly used survey research designs and their strengths and weaknesses.

Select one of the possible answers for each question.

Foundation level questions

1. Which of the following is a problem commonly associated with survey research?

    A. People often misinterpret or do not understand questions in the survey and therefore respond inaccurately.

    B. If asked about retrospective behaviour, people may have forgotten or remember incorrectly, leading to inaccurate responding.

    C. Some questions may be leading in nature, implying a specific response is desired from the participant, leading to inaccurate responding.

    D. All of the above.

Your answer:

2. What is a sampling frame?

    A. A list of members of the population of interest.

    B. A statistical technique for calculating the number of participants for a research study.

    C. A set of guidelines provided by a researcher to all individuals involved in the recruitment of participants to ensure they follow the same standardised procedure.

    D. All of these are examples of sampling frames.

Your answer:

3. A population distribution on gender is as follows: 40% male and 60% female. Which of the following samples would be representative of the population on this characteristic?

   A. 200 participants, comprising 120 males and 80 females.

   B. 200 participants, comprising 120 females and 80 males.

   C. 200 participants, comprising 100 female and 100 males.

   D. 200 participants, comprising 150 females and 50 males.

   Your answer: [ ]

4. A researcher is planning to use the phone book as a sampling frame for their research into consumer behaviour. What is a potential issue for this?

   A. Not everyone in the population will have a phone or have their phone number listed, so systematic bias will be introduced into the research.

   B. The phone book is too large to be a useful sampling frame – it will be unwieldy.

   C. There may be systematic bias in who phone numbers are registered to. For example, people are more likely to be adults, so adolescents may be under-represented.

   D. Both A and C.

   Your answer: [ ]

5. Which of the following is an example of a survey method?

   A. Postal surveys.

   B. Face-to-face interviews.

   C. Telephone interviews.

   D. All of the above.

   Your answer: [ ]

6. Which of the following is an example of a survey research design?

   A. Cross-sectional.

   B. Successive independent samples design.

   C. Longitudinal design.

   D. All of the above.

   Your answer: [A]

7. To what does 'discriminatory power' refer?

    A. The predictive power of a questionnaire.

    B. The impact of prejudice on the design of questionnaires.

    C. The ability of a questionnaire to differentiate between a wide variety of human responses, not just extremes.

    D. The power of a questionnaire to differentiate between truthful and dishonest participant responses.

Your answer: ☐

8. 'Equally appearing intervals' is an example of what?

    A. A response bias in participants' answers on a questionnaire.

    B. An attitude scale.

    C. A method of random sampling.

    D. None of the above.

Your answer: ☐

9. Respondents can answer in their own terms, responses are not prescribed and unexpected responses are more likely to be captured are characteristics associated with which type of question?

    A. Open questions.

    B. Closed questions.

    C. Implicit questions.

    D. Explicit questions.

Your answer: ☐

10. Some survey research involves showing participants a hypothetical situation and asking them to answer a set of questions based on it. The aim of such research is usually to examine people's perceptions and values, such as moral reasoning processes. This approach is commonly referred to as what?

    A. Elaborative.

    B. Scenario.

    C. Vignette.

    D. None of the above.

Your answer: ☐ C ✓

$\frac{8}{10}$

80%.

Advanced level questions

11. A low response rate to a survey indicates what?

   A. Response bias.

   B. Selection bias.

   C. Interviewer bias.

   D. None of the above.

Your answer: [A] □ x A

12. Which of the following refers to a survey research design which involves selecting one or more samples from the population at <u>one point in time</u>?

   A. Successive independent-samples design.

   B. Cross-sectional design.

   C. Longitudinal design.

   D. None of the above.

Your answer: [A]

13. To which research goals are cross-sectional surveys most suited?

   A. Descriptive.

   B. Inferring cause and effect.

   C. Predictive.

   D. Both A and C.

Your answer: [D]

14. With which survey research design is attrition a particular concern?

   A. Successive independent-samples design.

   B. Telephone interviews.

   C. Longitudinal.

   D. Cross-sectional.

Your answer: [C] ✓

15. Ethnicity, age and socio-economic status are all examples of what?

A. Demographic variables.

B. Master status.

C. Participant variables.

D. All of the above.

Your answer: ☐

16. Which of the following is an example of a double-barrelled item?

A. Abortion is a woman's choice and should be made freely available in supportive clinics.

B. People should fight institutional racism whenever they are confronted with it.

C. Indirect discrimination is just as bad as direct discrimination because it results in different groups within society being disadvantaged, which perpetuates inequality.

D. All of the above.

Your answer: ☐

17. The tendency for participants to agree to statements rather than disagree is referred to as what?

A. Sensitivity.

B. Demand characteristics.

C. Response acquiescence set.

D. Latency.

Your answer: ☐

18. Which of the following is a technique commonly used in psychometric test development to explore the underlying structure of a questionnaire?

A. Multiple regression.

 **B.** Factor analysis.

C. Factorial ANOVA.

D. Logistic regression.

Your answer: ☐

19. An attitude measure which involves studying responses that are thought to relate to attitudes rather than asking respondents to report their beliefs or evaluations is called what?

    A. Explicit measure.

    B. Direct measure.

    C. Indirect measure.

    D. Single-item measure.

Your answer: C ✓

20. Measuring attitudes using direct questions in survey research has not always been found to correlate highly with people's behaviour. For this reason, researchers such as Greenwald, McGhee and Schwartz (1998) have developed indirect measures to assess attitudes. Which of the following represents this approach to measuring attitudes?

    A. A multi-item measure.

    B. An implicit association test (IAT).

    C. A priming procedure.

    D. None of the above.

40 %

$\dfrac{12}{20}$

Your answer: B ✓

60 %

Extended multiple-choice question

Complete the following paragraph using the items listed below. Not all of the items will be consistent with the paragraph and not all items can be used. Items can be used only once.

Researchers designing a questionnaire can make use of a range of different _____. The most commonly used in psychological research is the Likert scale (Likert, 1932), also known as the _____ scale. This scale involves presenting the participant with a statement, which they are asked to record their attitude toward on a scale comprising an _____ number of _____ statements (e.g. strongly agree to strongly disagree). Each possible answer is associated with a unique number, which can then be used to calculate a mean for all items on that scale. The Likert scale is not without controversy, however; many researchers use the data derived from them as _____ data. However, other researchers argue that the data represents _____ measurement and therefore is not suitable for the same statistical procedures. Another type of response scale is the _____ (Osgood, Suci and Tannenbaum, 1957). These scales are formed so that there are two _____ and participants are invited to mark on the space between them where they feel their position toward the attitude object lies. This allows the respondent greater _____ in expressing how they feel, but is extremely hard to analyse, as different participants' responses are extremely unlikely to be _____.

Optional items

A. summated ratings

B. equal

C. bipolar adjectives

D. ordinal level

E. comparable

F. flexibility

G. cumulative scaling

H. easy and hard

I. semantic differential

J. interval level

K. response scales

L. ease

M. favourable and unfavourable

Essay questions for Chapter 7

Once you have completed the MCQs above you are ready to tackle some essay questions. You might like to select three or four topics and make notes on them. One way of doing this is to create a concept map. The first question has been done for you and you can see how the knowledge required links to some of the MCQs in this chapter.

1. Critically compare and evaluate the postal survey, internet survey and telephone interview approaches to survey research.

2. Critically examine the issues a researcher must consider when designing a questionnaire for survey research.

3. You are asked to design a research study exploring political beliefs using the postal survey method. Critically discuss the strategies you could use to make the research as effective as possible.

4. Discuss the difficulties involved in designing survey research to explore people's attitudes. What factors must a researcher consider to ensure the survey is as effective as possible?

5. Describe and evaluate the information a researcher would require in order to examine the reliability and validity of a questionnaire or psychometric test.

6. Describe and compare the successive independent samples design and the longitudinal survey design. What are the strengths and weaknesses of these two approaches?

7. Compare and evaluate the survey research and experimental research approaches to studying people's attitudes towards exercise.

8. Critically evaluate the strategies which researchers can use to increase the honesty and openness of participants' responses in survey research.

Chapter 7 essay question 1: concept map

Critically compare and evaluate the postal survey, internet survey and telephone interview approaches to survey research.

The concept map opposite provides an example of how the first sample essay may be conceptualised. Consideration of the different methods of conducting survey research identifies many subtopics, exploration of which will allow the strengths and weaknesses of different approaches to be evaluated. In this case the research suggests that although there are common themes for all survey methods, some issues apply more to one method of data collection than to others (e.g. interviewer bias). Further subtopics explore methods of mitigating or eliminating these issues (e.g. comparing respondents with non-responders) and provide insight into when each method can be most appropriately used.

Remember that it is important to link your answers to other topic areas not covered in this chapter.

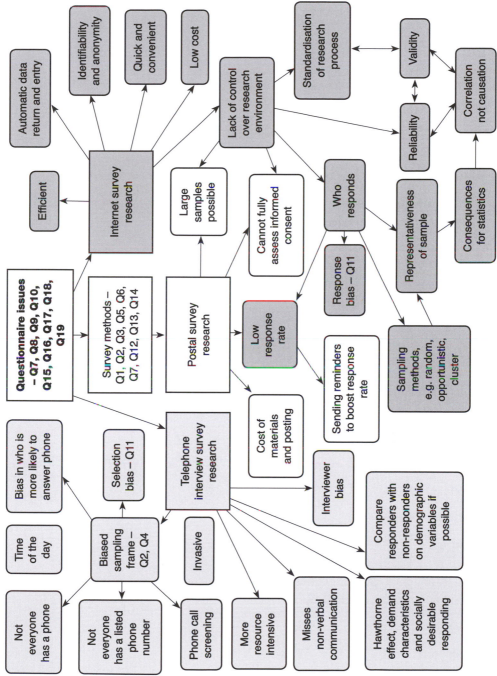

Chapter 8
Reliability and validity

This chapter includes questions on the different forms of reliability and validity, their implications for research and the methods used to assess them.

Select one of the possible answers for each question.

Foundation level questions

1. In observational research, the reliability or consistency of the application of a coding scheme over time is known as what?

    A. Inter-observer reliability.

    B. Intra-observer reliability.

    C. Predictive reliability.

    D. Criterion-related reliability.

    Your answer:

2. Which of the following is a validity concern relevant to structured observational research studies?

    A. Face validity.

    B. Concurrent validity.

    C. External validity.

    D. All of the above.

    Your answer:

3. What statistical analysis technique is most associated with the assessment of inter-observer consistency?

    A. Cronbach's alpha.

    B. Kappa.

    C. Chi-square.

    D. Correlation.

    Your answer:

4. What statistical analysis technique is most associated with the assessment of internal consistency of a questionnaire?

   A. Cronbach's alpha.

   B. Kappa.

   C. Chi-square.

   D. Correlation.

Your answer: A ✓

5. Which form of validity is concerned with the effectiveness of a test in predicting individuals' behaviour in specified situations, and can be established through comparison with another direct, independent measure designed to assess the same thing?

   A. Concurrent validity.

   B. Construct validity.

   C. Criterion-related validity.

   D. Face validity.

Your answer: A × C

6. Which form of validity, first proposed by Lawshe (1952), involves assessing the relationship between a composite score taken to represent all the underlying factors of a complex test (or battery of tests) and a measure of actual performance?

   A. Intrinsic validity.

   B. Synthetic validity.

   C. Nomological validity.

   D. Incremental validity.

Your answer: C × B

7. Using different methods of collecting data, sources of evidence and tests can help a researcher to be more confident in their research findings. What is this strategy called?

   A. Construct validity.

   B. Discriminant validity.

   C. Triangulation.

   D. Experimental control.

Your answer: A × C

8. Which of the following statements is incorrect?

    A. If a questionnaire is shown to be valid and reliable with the group it was developed with, it will automatically be valid and reliable with other groups of people too.

    B. If a questionnaire is shown to be valid and reliable in one context it will automatically be valid and reliable in other contexts.

    C. If a questionnaire is shown to be valid and reliable for the purpose it was intended, it will automatically be valid and reliable for use with other purposes.

    D. All of the above.

Your answer: A × B

9. Which of the following would you not expect to achieve high test-retest reliability?

    A. Religious orientation.

    B. Personality.

    C. Mood.

    D. Intelligence.

Your answer: C × D

10. If scores on a stress questionnaire administered on two separate occasions a month apart are significantly different, what does this imply?

    A. The test may have poor test-retest reliability.

    B. Something may have happened in the month between test administrations to alter participants' scores.

    C. The conditions under which the tests were administered may have been significantly different, therefore affect participants' responses.

    D. All of the above.

Your answer: D × B

$$\frac{7}{10}$$ 70%

Advanced level questions

11. Which of the following is likely to increase the reliability of a questionnaire?

   A. Ensuring all items in the questionnaire fit well with one another.

   B. Using multiple-items to assess a construct.

   C. Using uniform testing procedures.

   D. All of the above.

Your answer: ☐ D ✓

12. Construct validity can be subdivided into two further concepts. What are they?

   A. Convergent validity and divergent validity.

   B. Predictive validity and criterion-related validity.

   C. Convergent validity and discriminant validity.

   D. External validity and internal validity.

Your answer: ☐ D ✗

13. Which of the following statements is true?

   A. A measure may be valid but not reliable.

   B. A measure may be reliable but not valid.

   C. Both A and B.

   D. None of the above.

Your answer: ☐ C ✗

14. Which of the following best indicates the reliability of a questionnaire?

   A. The spread of scores on the test.

   B. The extent to which scores on the test correlate with a different measure assessing the same construct.

   C. The consistency of scores on repeated administrations of the test.

   D. The degree to which scores on the test form a normal distribution.

Your answer: ☐ C ✓

15. The American Psychological Association differentiates between which two types of validity, based on the time relations between obtaining the test scores and obtaining a criterion measure?

   A. Construct and predictive.

   B. Concurrent and predictive.

   C. Convergent and discriminant.

   D. Convergent and construct.

   Your answer:  D × B

16. Which statistical analysis technique is particularly useful for assessing construct validity?

   A. Logistic regression.

   B. Multiple regression.

   C. Factorial ANOVA.

   D. Factor analysis.

   Your answer: B × D

17. Campbell (1960) argued that to demonstrate a test is valid it is not enough merely to show that the test correlates highly with variables that it should theoretically correlate with. It is also necessary to demonstrate that the test does not correlate significantly with variables with which it is not expected to. What is this latter form of validity?

   A. Diametrical.

   B. Differential.

   C. Discriminant.

   D. Divergent.

   Your answer: C ✓

18. Which of the following is the most basic form of validity analysis?

   A. Concurrent validity.

   B. Face validity.

   C. Content validity.

   D. Convergent validity.

   Your answer: B ✓

19. When investigating test-retest reliability there is a potential for practice effects. What method can be used to assess test-retest reliability, which avoids this issue?

    A. Kuder-Richardson reliability.

    B. Alternate-form reliability.

    C. Split-half reliability.

    D. Intra-rater reliability.

Your answer: _C_ ✗

20. If it is not feasible to conduct research into the predictive validity of a test, for example it is not practically possible to allow for the time required to validate the measure on the criterion variable, what other form of validity assessment is often carried out in its place?

    A. Concurrent. _does a_ _but say w/ an nothing_

    B. Convergent.

    C. Discriminant.

    D. Synthetic.

Your answer: _D_ ✗

Extended multiple-choice question

Complete the following paragraph using the items listed overleaf. Not all of the items will be consistent with the paragraph and not all items can be used. Items can be used only once.

The term '_____' is often applied in a different way to qualitative psychological research than to quantitative psychological research, owing to _____ and ontological differences between the two approaches. For this reason _____ (1985) suggest that rather than 'validity', qualitative researchers should explore the degree of '_____' of their data. According to these authors, this construct comprises four concepts: confirmability, transferability, credibility and dependability. _____ refers to the evaluation of whether or not the findings from research offer a reasonable and plausible interpretation of the data collected. _____ refers to the degree to which the findings of the research can be applied outside the boundaries of the specific study in question. _____ refers to the assessment of the quality of the data collection, data analysis and theory generation processes carried out during the research. Finally, _____ refers to an assessment of the extent to which the research findings are actually supported by the data collected. This approach also highlights the different role that the concept of '_____' plays in qualitative research compared to quantitative research. For example, qualitative research often makes use of the _____ method. In this type of research the emphasis is placed on exploring the _____ dynamics of the specific individual or organisation selected for the research, rather than attempting to _____ research findings to a wider group of people. Therefore representativeness is not an issue in this situation. However, although qualitative research often employs small, 'unrepresentative' samples, there may be instances in which generalisation of an observed experience is desirable. In these situations qualitative researchers often make use of _____ techniques, such as checking an experience in one context against _____ experiences in other contexts.

Optional items

A. representativeness

B. similar

C. different

D. Glaser and Strauss

E. trustworthiness

F. transferability

G. accumulative

H. generalise

I. epistemological

J. quality

K. credibility

L. Lincoln and Guba

M. validity

N. dependability

O. survey

P. internal

Q. confirmability

R. case study

Essay questions for Chapter 8

Once you have completed the MCQs above you are ready to tackle some essay questions. You might like to select three or four topics and make notes on them. One way of doing this is to create a concept map. The first question has been done for you and you can see how the knowledge required links to some of the MCQs in this chapter.

1. Critically discuss what is meant by the term 'valid measure'.

2. Critically examine the considerations involved in designing a psychometric test of personality.

3. Critically examine the ways in which the processes for establishing the validity and reliability of survey research compare with experimental research.

4. In what ways do the concepts of reliability and validity interrelate? Provide examples of contemporary psychological research to illustrate your answer.

5. Discuss the procedures which could be used for establishing the ecological validity of a laboratory experiment.

6. Compare the different approaches to assessing reliability and validity in quantitative and qualitative research. Provide examples of psychological research to illustrate your answer.

7. You are asked to design a self-report measure of work-style orientation, for an organisation to use as part of their recruitment selection processes. It is proposed that a greater degree of task-oriented work-style will result in greater success within the organisation. Critically discuss how you could strive to ensure the questionnaire was a valid and reliable measure.

8. Providing examples of research to illustrate your answer, critically examine the impact of sampling methods and research designs on the reliability and validity of survey research findings.

Chapter 8 essay question 1: concept map

Critically discuss what is meant by the term 'valid measure'.

The concept map opposite provides an example of how the first sample essay may be conceptualised. Consideration of the different epistemological and ontological positions underpinning different research perspectives (e.g. quantitative and qualitative) leads to several subtopics, which should be critically evaluated before conclusions can be drawn. Examining these subtopics allows for a fuller understanding of the different conceptualisations of validity (e.g. construct validity vs. trustworthiness), the implications this has for the emphasis placed upon it in different research, and how validity can be assessed. The topic of reliability is also brought into discussion, which is strongly related to the concept of validity and has implications for the aims and scope of different 'measures' in psychological research.

Remember that it is important to link your answers to other topic areas not covered in this chapter.

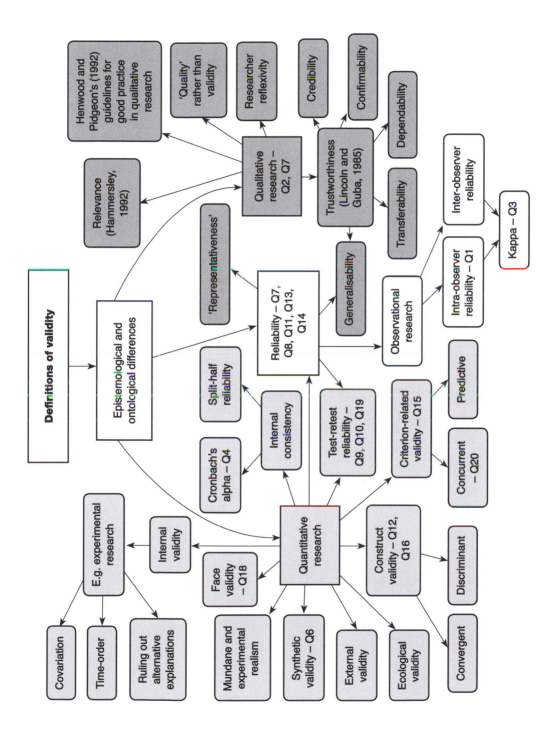

Chapter 9
Qualitative approaches and methods

This chapter covers qualitative approaches to psychological research, including questions on phenomenology and discursive psychology, common methods of data collection and analysis and their associated strengths and weaknesses.

Select one of the possible answers for each question.

Foundation level questions

1. Willig (2008) argues that many qualitative researchers tend not to work with 'variables' that are defined by the researcher prior to the research process because:

   A. It imposes the researcher's meanings on the phenomenon.

   B. The aim of much qualitative research is not to predict but to explore, so 'variables' are not very useful constructs.

   C. It prevents the respondent from making sense of a phenomenon for themselves.

   D. All of the above.

   Your answer:  B ✓

2. Which of the following activities is not associated with the grounded theory method of data analysis?

   A. Constant comparative analysis.

   B. Q-method.

   C. Theoretical sampling.

   D. Theoretical saturation.

   Your answer: ⬜ B ✓

3. Which of the following texts would not be appropriate for conversation analysis?

    A. Transcription of an interview conducted by the researcher.

    B. Transcription of a televised political debate between MPs.

    C. Notes written by an interviewer during the course of an interview.

    D. None of the above.

Your answer: ☐ ✓ C ✓

4. According to Willig (2008), what is the most widely used method of data collection in qualitative psychological research?

    A. Semi-structured interview.

    B. Unstructured interview.

    C. Participant observation.

    D. Natural observation.

Your answer: ☐ A ✓

5. What did Gail Jefferson develop?

    A. A form of analysis for pictorial objects.

    B. A form of categorising interview quotations.

    C. A form of transcription notation.

    D. A form of quality assessment for interview data.

Your answer: ☐ ✓ B C ✓

6. In focus groups the researcher typically takes which role?

    A. Leader.

    B. Participant.

    C. Moderator.

    D. 'Devil's advocate'.

Your answer: ☐ C ✓

7. Jonathan Smith (1997) founded which movement?

A. Genetic phenomenology.

B. Hermeneutical phenomenology.

C. Existential phenomenology.

D. Interpretative phenomenological analysis.

Your answer: ☐ D ✓

8. Willig (2008) suggests that qualitative methodologies can be differentiated by the differing emphasis they place on what?

A. Reflexivity and the role of language.

B. Reflexivity and degree of researcher participation in research.

C. The role of language and degree of researcher participation in research.

D. Generalisability and degree of objectivity.

Your answer: ☐ A ✓

9. The concept of 'intentionality', is associated with which approach to research?

A. Ethnomethodology.

B. Transcendental phenomenology.

C. Discursive psychology.

D. Grounded theory.

Your answer: ☐ B ✓

10. To ensure all participants remain actively involved in discussion, Willig (2008) suggests that focus groups should comprise no more than how many participants?

A. 6.

B. 7.

C. 8.

D. 9.

Your answer: ☐ ✓

A ✓

Advanced level questions

11. In what ways do transcendental phenomenology and the use of the phenomenological method in psychology differ?

    A. They differ over whether emphasis should be on introspective contemplation of the researcher's experience of a phenomenon or on exploration of the research participants' account of an event as the phenomenon.

    B. They differ over whether the focus should be on the diversity and variability of human experience or on the identification essences.

    C. They differ over whether researchers should strive to fully suspend biases or be reflexive.

    D. All of the above.

    Your answer: [ ] D ~~A~~ ✓

12. In grounded theory, what are concepts?

    A. Descriptive labels.

    B. Linkages between categories.

    C. Analytical labels.

    D. Both A and C.

    Your answer: [A]

↓ sociology concepts grounded
↓ examining data in

13. Ideally, which of the following descriptions should apply to category labels in grounded theory?

    A. They should be developed from the text in such a way that the categories appear mutually exclusive.

    B. They should be derived from words or phrases used by the respondents themselves (in vivo). ✓

    C. They should be characterised by a new descriptive phrase which has not already been used in participants' responses.

    D. Both A and C.

    Your answer: [B]

14. Axial coding, as proposed by Strauss and Corbin (1990), is a coding paradigm that explicitly focuses on identifying what in the data?

   A. Manifestations of 'process' and 'change'.

   B. Expressions of emotion.

   C. 'Negative cases'.

   D. Symbols and representations.

Your answer: A ✓ A B

15. What is negative case analysis in grounded theory?

   A. Looking for instances in which the participant contradicts themselves.

   B. Looking for examples of 'opposites'.

   C. Looking for instances that do not fit with categories and linkages.

   D. All of these are examples of negative case analysis in grounded theory.

Your answer: D ✗ C

16. The practice of asking questions of the data in grounded theory, and modifying emerging categories, ideas, concepts and linkage constructs as a result, is known as what?

   A. Theoretical sensitivity.

   B. Theoretical sampling.

   C. Theoretical saturation.

   D. Memo-writing.

Your answer: C ✗ A

17. Prior to the research process in grounded theory research, what should a researcher do?

   A. Never have research questions prior to the research process.

   B. Identify an open, descriptive research question prior to the research process.

   C. Identify a research question that is as narrow and specific as possible.

   D. Use constructs from existing theories to inform the research question.

Your answer: D ✗ B

18. What does the 'abbreviated' version of grounded theory refer to?

    A. Using the original method of grounded theory, which does not employ axial coding.

    B. Using grounded theory as a method of data analysis only, not an approach to research.

    C. Grounded theory analysis which does not strive for theoretical saturation.

    D. None of the above.

Your answer: B ✓

19. Why is the Jefferson method of transcription the most popular?

    A. It attempts to capture 'talk' as it is heard.

    B. It captures the interactivity of 'talk', as is necessary for performing an adequate interactional analysis.

    C. It provides enough detail to allow other researchers to fully check the claims made by a researcher, even if the analysis is concerned with features of lexical content.

    D. All of the above.

Your answer: D ✓

20. Which of the following is not a stage in interpretative phenomenological analysis?

    A. Labelling themes.

    B. Clustering themes.

    C. Fractionating themes.

    D. Production of a summary table.

Your answer: A ✗

Extended multiple-choice question

Complete the following paragraph using the items listed below. Not all of the items will be consistent with the paragraph and not all items can be used. Items can be used only once.

Hammersley (1966) proposed a classification for approaches to ___qualitative___ [×A] research, and identified three key approaches to research which combines ___K___ ✓ and ___E___ ✓ research. The first approach is called ___D___ ✓, which refers to the use of quantitative research to ___G×L___ qualitative research findings, or qualitative research to corroborate quantitative research findings. The second approach is called ___J___ ✓, which refers to the situation in which one research strategy is employed in order to ___H___ [×A] research using the other research strategy. The third approach identified is termed ___A×L___. This approach is used when two research strategies are employed in order that different aspects of an investigation can be ___C___ ✓ together.

Optional items

A. multi-strategy

B. disprove

C. married

D. triangulation

E. quantitative

F. refute

G. aid

H. corroborate

I. differentiated

J. facilitation

K. qualitative

L. complementarity

Essay questions for Chapter 9

Once you have completed the MCQs above you are ready to tackle some essay questions. You might like to select three or four topics and make notes on them. One way of doing this is to create a concept map. The first question has been done for you and you can see how the knowledge required links to some of the MCQs in this chapter.

1. Husserl argued that it is possible to fully suspend your presuppositions and beliefs when considering a phenomenon. Critically discuss the extent to which you agree with this claim?

2. Critically evaluate the concept of small-q and big-Q research (Kidder and Fine, 1987). In what ways might they interpret the same phenomena differently?

3. Some researchers, such as Hammersley, argue that qualitative and quantitative research methodologies can be combined, while other researchers view the two as being mutually exclusive. Critically discuss this debate, providing evidence for your position.

4. To what extent are the concepts of 'representativeness' and 'generalisability' issues for qualitative research?

5. Critically examine the role of 'language' in qualitative research.

6. 'Qualitative and quantitative researchers are attempting to answer the same questions in psychology and are simply using different methods to do so.' Discuss this suggestion providing examples of psychological theory and research.

7. The goal of psychology should be to discover universal laws underlying human behaviour. To what extent do you agree with this position? Provide examples of research and theory to support your argument.

8. Compare the grounded theory analysis and discursive psychology approaches to research. Critically examine the ways in which they might interpret the same phenomena differently.

Chapter 9 essay question 1: concept map

Husserl argued that it is possible to fully suspend your presuppositions and beliefs when considering a phenomenon. Critically discuss the extent to which you agree with this claim.

The concept map below provides an example of how the first sample essay may be conceptualised. Consideration of the different epistemological and ontological positions underpinning Objectivism and Interpretivism leads to several subtopics, which need to be critically evaluated before conclusions can be drawn. Examining these subtopics will explore the differing aims of researchers working in Discursive Psychology and Empiricism, for example. Therefore, the extent to which this claim is believed will depend largely on whether the researcher believes that *impartiality* or *involvement* is necessary to research the phenomenon in question.

Remember that it is important to link your answers to other topic areas not covered in this chapter.

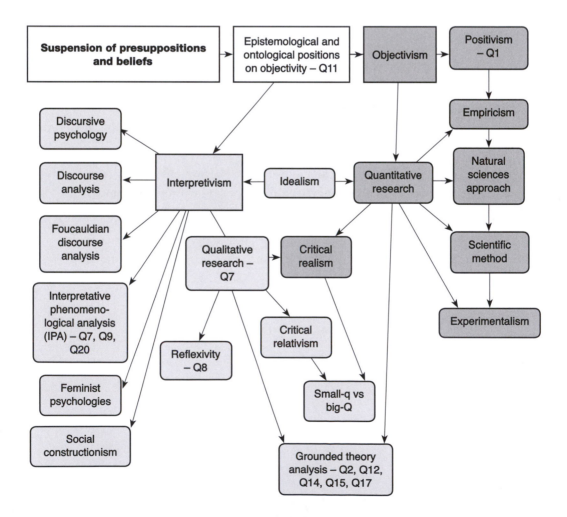

Chapter 10
Ethics of research with humans and animals

This chapter covers the ethical issues psychological researchers must consider when working with human participants and non-human animal participants, including the ethical guidelines to which psychologists must adhere, the organisations which produce ethical guidelines and regulate practice and research, and the implications these have for research in psychology.

Select one of the possible answers for each question.

Foundation level questions

1. In order to offer services to the public as a psychology practitioner in the UK, with which organisation must an individual be registered?

   A. British Psychology Society (BPS).

   B. Health Professions Council (HPC).

   C. National Health Service (NHS).

   D. All of the above.

   Your answer: D ⨯ B

2. A conflict between different principles of moral conduct is known as what?

   A. An ethical conundrum.

   B. An ethical dilemma.

   C. An ethical catastrophe.

   D. An ethical dispute.

   Your answer: B ✓

3. To whom does the British Psychological Society's code of ethics and conduct (2009) apply?

   A. All psychology students.

   B. All psychology lecturers, researchers and practitioners.

   C. All members and student affiliates of the BPS.

   D. Everyone in the UK.

Your answer: C   ✓

4. The BPS suggests that level of identifiability and level of observation form the basis of the additional ethical issues in which of the following?

   A. Research in prisons.

   B. Research with animals.

   C. Research on the Internet.

   D. Research with all human participants.

Your answer: D   ✗ C

5. Which of the lists below contains the four general ethical principles of the British Psychological Society?

   A. Respect, beneficence, responsibility and integrity.

   B. Respect, non-maleficence, fidelity and integrity.

   C. Respect, competence, responsibility and integrity.

   D. Justice, competence, beneficence and non-maleficence.

Your answer: C   ✗ D

6. What is the purpose of informed consent?

   A. To ensure participants are fully aware of the time commitment they should expect for the research.

   B. To ensure participants have enough information to be able to make an informed choice about whether they want to participate in the research or not and that they know they can withdraw at any point in the process.

   C. To ensure participants are aware of what participation in the research will entail.

   D. All of the above.

Your answer: D   ✓

7. Deliberately fabricating details of a research project is known as what?

   A. Lying by commission.

   B. Lying by omission.

   C. Lying by fabrication.

   D. Lying by invention.

Your answer:  A ✗

8. Which of the following statements is correct?

   A. Only research carried out by academic staff and students involving face-to-face interaction with participants requires ethical approval.

   B. All research carried out by academic staff and students, regardless of whether there is face-to-face interaction with participants or not, requires ethical approval.

   C. Only research conducted by academic staff requires ethical approval.

   D. Only research conducted by academic staff and students with human participants requires ethical approval.

Your answer:  ✓

9. Which type of research does the BPS suggest involves 'additional' ethical considerations, because of the nature of the research restricting the researcher's ability to monitor, support and terminate the research if adverse reactions become apparent?

   A. Research on the Internet.

   B. Research with animals.

   C. Research with participants not having the ability to consent to their participation.

   D. Research in prisons.

Your answer: C ✗

10. There are two broad perspectives regarding the application of ethical principles in psychological research. One perspective suggests that ethical principles should never be broken whereas the other perspective suggests that the transgression of ethical principles should be considered on a case-by-case basis. What are these two perspectives commonly referred to as?

   A. Globalist and situationist.

   B. Globalist and contextualist.

   C. Universalist and situationist.

   D. Universalist and contextualist.

Your answer: [C] ✓

Advanced level questions

11. A researcher has completed 20, one-hour-long semi-structured interviews and has just finished transcribing them when a research participant contacts him to say they want to withdraw from the study. Removing the participant's data from the research would mean a considerable loss of information which took a long period of time to collect and transcribe. What should the researcher do?

   A. Contact the participant for a follow-up interview to see why they want to withdraw from the study.

   B. Tell the participant that it's too late because the data has been transcribed and data analysis has already started.

   C. All information contributed by that participant up to that date should be destroyed or turned over to the participant for them to destroy.

   D. All of the above responses are acceptable.

Your answer: [A] ✗

12. Where are the ethical guidelines for Internet research provided by the British Psychological Society located?

    A. On the BPS's main website.

    B. Internet and other forms of research are not differentiated by the BPS.

    C. In a separate supplemental publication to the code of ethics and conduct (2009) available from the BPS.

    D. In a separate stand-alone publication to the code of ethics and conduct (2009) available from the BPS.

Your answer: C ✓

13. The BPS publishes division-specific professional practice guidelines as well as the generic professional guidelines. Which of the following divisions does not currently have its own professional practice guidelines published?

    A. Division of neuropsychology.

    B. Division for teachers and researchers in psychology.

    C. Division of educational and child psychology.

    D. Division of counselling psychology.

Your answer: D ✗

14. Which of the following is a legislative act covering the ethical use of animals in psychological research in the UK?

    A. Animals (Research Procedures) Act 1986.

    B. Animals (Scientific Procedures) Act 1986.

    C. Animals (Experimentation Procedures) Act 1986.

    D. Animals (Vivisection Procedures) Act 1986.

Your answer: A ✗

15. The Animals (Scientific Procedures) Act 1986 and the Animal Welfare Act (2006) both provide legislation in the UK concerned with the welfare of 'protected' animals. What are 'protected animals'?

A. All non-human vertebrates and a single invertebrate species.

B. All non-human vertebrates and invertebrate species.

C. All non-human vertebrates and invertebrate species commonly kept as pets.

D. All non-human vertebrate species commonly kept as pets.

Your answer:

16. Which of the following is *not* one of the three 'Rs' proposed by Russell and Burch (1959) relating to the considerations psychologists must demonstrate that they have made when requesting to use animals in regulated procedures?

A. *Replacing* animals with non-sentient alternatives whenever possible.

B. *Reducing* the number of animals.

C. *Refining* procedures to minimise suffering.

D. *Regulating* pain medication to ease animals' suffering.

Your answer:

17. To carry out a research project which involves regulated procedures on protected animals requires a _____ licence, which details the species of animal, numbers of animals and combinations of procedures that may be used. Each person who actually performs the regulated procedures must also have a _____ licence, which is given after the individual has completed appropriate training in the procedures.

A. Establishment, scientist's.

B. Research, private.

C. Project, personal.

D. Experimentation, experimenter's.

Your answer:

18. The BPS has published supplemental guidelines for best practice in IMR. What does this abbreviation stand for?

    A. Internet mediated research.

    B. Interpersonal management of relationships.

    C. Internally managed research.

    D. Investigative market research.

Your answer: A ✓

19. Which of the following is an ethical consideration faced by researchers when using financial incentives for research participation?

    A. Participants may feel unable to withdraw from the study if they accept a financial reward for agreeing to participate.

    B. This may increase the power imbalance between research participant and researcher.

    C. Participants may feel obligated to behave in a way they think the researcher wants them to behave.

    D. All of the above.

Your answer: D ✓

20. Which of the following is an issue associated with citing research such as that conducted by Milgram (1963) or Zimbardo (1973) to illustrate ethical issues in psychological research?

    A. They were conducted too long ago to be relevant today.

    B. It suggests that ethical issues only arise in extreme cases.

    C. It suggests that ethical issues only arise within certain cultures.

    D. It suggests that ethical issues only arise from using deception.

Your answer: A ✗ B

Extended multiple-choice question

Complete the following paragraphs using the items listed opposite. Not all of the items will be consistent with the paragraph and not all items can be used. Items can be used only once.

The term '___[informed]_ ___[consent]_ ✓' refers to the explicit statement of a person's willingness to participate in a research study, which is based on a clear understanding of the ___[nature of research]_ ✓, who is conducting the research, what the participant can expect if they choose to take part and any consequences they should be aware of if they do not take part. Key information that should be provided includes the fact that participation is ___[voluntary]_ ✓ and the participant can withdraw at ___[any time]_ ✓ without having to provide a reason. The ___[contact details]_ ✓ for the researcher/research team (so that participants can ask further questions about the study) should be provided, as well as information about sources of support should the participant require it and also information about how they can make ___[complaint]_ ✓.

There are a number of difficulties which researchers encounter when trying to obtain informed consent. For example, the ___[ID?]_ ___[anon?]_ of participants and confidentiality of their data must be ensured. Informed consent is also difficult to establish with specific methodologies, such as ___[capacity]_ [✗ internet research] (where the researcher cannot be certain that a participant is really of the required age or fully understands the information they have read) and ___[ethnomethod]_ ✓ (where the diverse range of people observed, for example, means that informed consent is difficult to obtain – particularly if employing covert observational methods). Another issue concerns individuals who do not have the ___[capacity]_ ✓ to consent to their participation, such as children and ___[vuln. adults]_ ✓. In these circumstances, researchers may seek to obtain informed consent from the individual's ___[legal ?]_ ✓ such as a parent. Therefore, it is important to recognise that obtaining informed consent is more than a participant deciding to take part in research; it is a reciprocal process whereby the researcher must also be in a position to judge the ___[quality]_ of a potential participant's decision. [capacity] [9 ans]

Optional items

A. anonymity

B. identifiability

C. voluntary

D. nature of the research

E. legal guardian

F. an official complaint

G. capacity

H. any time

I. vulnerable adults

J. quality

K. time

L. at the start of the research project

M. Internet research

N. extremely important

O. ethnomethodology

P. informed consent

Q. contact details

R. busy adults

Essay questions for Chapter 10

Once you have completed the MCQs above you are ready to tackle some essay questions. You might like to select three or four topics and make notes on them. One way of doing this is to create a concept map. The first question has been done for you and you can see how the knowledge required links to some of the MCQs in this chapter.

1. Discuss how ethical guidelines and codes of conduct protect participants, researchers and the wider community. Highlight contemporary debates within psychology to illustrate your answer.

2. If the format of *Big Brother*, the TV show, was in fact a psychological experiment, what ethical issues might there be? Critically examine the strategies which could be used to overcome these issues.

3. 'The code of conduct and ethics hinders psychological research into interesting phenomena.' Critically examine this position and provide examples of psychological research to support your argument.

4. What are the ethical concerns regarding the conduct of psychological research with animals? Critically discuss how these concerns can be mitigated.

5. If Stanley Milgram's electric shock study of obedience were proposed as a research project today, do you think it would obtain ethical approval? Explain your answer and discuss the implications of this posed for contemporary psychological research.

6. What ethical issues might arise for a researcher carrying out participant observation into gang-related car theft crime in London?

7. Critically examine the ethical issues which may arise for research conducted into dating preferences in offline and online environments.

8. What are the ethical concerns of conducting research with children and vulnerable adults? Critically discuss how these concerns can be mitigated.

Chapter 10 essay question 1: concept map

Discuss how ethical guidelines and codes of conduct protect participants, researchers and the wider community. Highlight contemporary debates within psychology to illustrate your answer.

The concept map overleaf provides an example of how the first sample essay may be conceptualised. Consideration of the ethical principles to which psychologists must adhere (for example, as outlined by the British Psychological Society in 2009), leads to several subtopics identifying methodological issues which subsequently arise. Examining examples of ethical issues in real-world research and the methods of mitigating/ eliminating ethical issues employed by researchers will provide a fuller understanding of the issues involved in planning and conducting research, and ultimately how this affects the wider community.

Remember that it is important to link your answers to other topic areas not covered in this chapter.

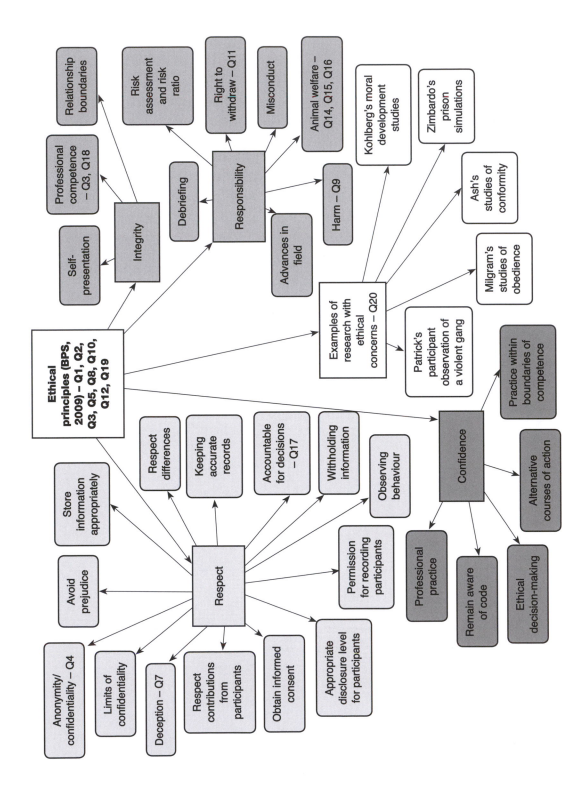

Chapter 11
Reporting research

This chapter explores best practice in report writing and includes questions on searching for relevant research, accepting and rejecting the null hypothesis and alternative hypothesis, reporting statistical analysis appropriately, referencing systems and referencing appropriately, structuring a research report and the publication of research.

Select one of the possible answers for each question.

Foundation level questions

1. What information should *not* be included in a results section?

   A. Description of descriptive and inferential statistical procedures used.

   B. Results of statistical analyses.

   C. Tables and/or graphs illustrating results.

   D. Details of the implications of analyses.

   Your answer: ☐

2. When do Shaughnessy, Zechmeister and Zechmeister (2009) suggest is often the best time to write the abstract for a research report?

   A. Before writing the main body of the research report.

   B. As you are writing the main body of the research report.

   C. After writing the main body of the research report.

   D. During the completion of each phase of the research process.

   Your answer: ☐

3. According to the publication manual of the American Psychological Association (2007), an abstract should not exceed what word limit?

   A. 120.

   B. 220.

   C. 320.

   D. 420.

   Your answer: ☐

4. You are writing a report in APA format and wish to cite an author's work which you have read about in another paper. Which of the following should you do?

   A. You should only reference the article you have actually read: reference the article of interest and indicate the source from which it was obtained.

   B. You should reference the article as if you have read the original paper.

   C. Either of the methods of referencing above are acceptable.

   D. You cannot cite the article at all unless you are able to obtain a copy of the original source.

   Your answer:

5. The term 'publication bias' refers to what?

   A. When an author appears to be ideologically biased in the way they have reported their results in a journal article or book.

   B. The difference between published research and unpublished research. For example, research papers reporting significant results are more likely to be published than research not reporting significant results.

   C. The fact that most authors prefer to submit their articles for publication in peer-reviewed journals.

   D. All of the above are examples of publication bias.

   Your answer:

6. What can a 'bibliographic index' be used for?

   A. Storing your research notes relating to journal articles.

   B. Obtaining access to full-text journal articles.

   C. Obtaining previews of academic reference texts.

   D. Searching a database of references to locate potentially useful literature.

   Your answer:

7. Which of the following is an example of a Boolean operator, which can be used to search electronic databases, bibliographic indexes and search engines, to help refine literature search criteria?

A. And.

B. Or.

C. Not.

D. All of the above.

Your answer: ☐

8. The British Psychological Society uses which referencing system in their research journals?

A. American Psychological Association (APA).

B. Harvard system.

C. Vancouver system.

D. Alpha-numeric.

Your answer: ☐

9. Which of the following is *not* one of the three types of ethnographic writing distinguished by Van Maanen (1988)?

A. Realist tales.

B. Confessional tales.

C. Impressionist tales.

D. Narrative tales.

Your answer: ☐

10. The structure of a research article reporting the findings of a qualitative study may be affected by what?

A. The role which extant theory plays in the research process.

B. The emphasis placed on verbatim quotes from research respondents.

C. The steps involved in performing the data analysis.

D. All of the above.

Your answer: ☐

Advanced level questions

11. What does it mean if an article is published in a 'refereed' journal?

  A. The article has been peer reviewed by experts in the specific field of research addressed in the paper.

  B. Authors can only contribute to the article if they are first approached by the journal's editor and asked to do so.

  C. The journal only publishes research deemed to be within the scientific sphere.

  D. The author of the article must supply employment references when submitting to the journal.

Your answer:

12. Which of the following is true about the objectives for an introduction?

  A. A literature review should introduce the problem being studied and indicate why the problem is an important one to study.

  B. A literature review should briefly summarise the relevant background literature related to the study to describe the theoretical implications of the study.

  C. A literature review should describe the purpose or rationale of the research and develop the predictions or hypotheses guiding the research.

  D. All of the above.

Your answer:

13. What are RefWorks and EndNote examples of?

  A. Bibliographic software.

  B. Journal article databases.

  C. Website bookmark managers.

  D. RSS feeds.

Your answer:

14. Which of the following is correct regarding the section reporting the results of a quantitative research study?

A. You should 'eyeball' data prior to inferential statistical analysis and suggest where differences or correlations might arise.

B. You should provide the underlying details of the inferential statistical procedure adopted, such as its rationale or the formula used to calculate the significance of the test.

C. You should include sufficient information in the results section to enable someone reading your paper to reach their own conclusions about the implications of your data.

D. It is acceptable for a results section to comprise solely tables, figures and statistical results.

Your answer:

15. In a research study the relationship between 30 participants' scores on a measure of stress (higher scores indicate higher levels of stress) and a measure of exercise frequency (higher scores indicate greater frequency of exercise) were assessed using Pearson's correlation coefficient. The following statistical result was quoted: $r = -0.63$, $p < 0.5$. Assuming the data was appropriate for this statistical procedure used and there are no confounding variables identified, which of the following is an appropriate interpretation of this statistical result?

A. There is a significant positive correlation between participants' scores on the measure of stress and the frequency with which they exercise, suggesting that as participants exercise more frequently, scores on the measure of stress increase.

B. There is a significant positive correlation between participants' scores on the measure of stress and the frequency with which they exercise, suggesting that as participants exercise more frequently, scores on the measure of stress decrease.

C. There is a significant negative correlation between participants' scores on the measure of stress and the frequency with which they exercise, suggesting that as participants exercise more frequently, scores on the measure of stress decrease.

D. There is no significant correlation between participants' scores on the measure of stress and the frequency with which they exercise.

Your answer:

16. Which of the following is an example of reporting the result of a chi-square (χ^2) test of independence, in APA format?

  A. χ^2 = value (degrees of freedom), significance, e.g. χ^2 = 6.25 (3), p <0.05.

  B. χ^2 (degrees of freedom, sample size) = value, significance,
    e.g. χ^2 (3, N = 50) = 6.25, p < 0.05.

  C. χ^2 = value (sample size), significance, e.g. χ^2 = 6.25 (N = 50), p < 0.05.

  D. χ^2 = value (degrees of freedom, sample size), significance, e.g. χ^2 = 6.25 (3, N = 50), p < 0.05.

Your answer: [ ]

17. Which of the following points, broadly applying to all forms of qualitative research, did Burnard (2004) suggest should be considered when writing qualitative research reports (particularly for publication)?

  A. They should include a 'findings' section, not a 'results' section.

  B. They should be careful not to generalise beyond the data.

  C. They should consider whether it is more appropriate to present the findings of the analysis separately from supporting discussion, or should link the findings of the analysis to the work of other researchers simultaneously.

  D. All of the above.

Your answer: [ ]

18. The APA publication manual encourages the results of regression analyses to be reported with the aid of tables. Complete the following paragraph using the options provided.
When presenting the results of a regression analysis in a table, both the raw/unstandardised coefficients (_) and standardised coefficients (_) should be included, unless the study is purely applied (in which case only the _____ coefficients should be listed) or purely theoretical (in which case only the _____ coefficients should be listed).

  A. B, β, raw/unstandardised, standardised.

  B. B, B, raw/unstandardised, standardised.

  C. B, β, raw/unstandardised, standardised.

  D. A, α, standardised, raw/unstandardised.

Your answer: [ ]

19. When compiling a reference list, which of the following formats is correct when referencing a chapter in an edited book in the Harvard referencing system format?

   A. Bloggs, J.D. (2011) The benefits of MCQs. In: Other, N.E. (ed.) *Revising successfully*. London, University Press, pp. 1–10.

   B. Bloggs, J.D. 2011. The benefits of MCQs. In Other, N.E. (Ed.), *Revising successfully* (Ch. 2.). London: University Press.

   C. Bloggs, J.D. (2011). The benefits of MCQs. In N.E. Other (Ed.), *Revising successfully* (pp. 1–10). London: University Press.

   D. All of the above are acceptable.

Your answer:

20. Tong, Sainsbury and Craig (2007) developed COREQ: what is the official name of this tool and what does it aim to assist researchers with?

   A. Consolidated criteria for observational research questions – a 32-item checklist for developing feasible, appropriately defined research questions with observational research.

   B. Consolidated criteria for reporting quasi-experimental research – a 32-item checklist for reporting research from quasi-experiments such as natural experiments.

   C. Consolidated criteria for reporting qualitative research – a 32-item checklist for reporting research from interviews and focus groups.

   D. Consolidated criteria for research quality – a 32-item checklist for researchers as a tool when designing studies.

Your answer:

Extended multiple-choice question

Complete the following paragraph using the items listed overleaf. Not all of the items will be consistent with the paragraph and not all items can be used. Items can be used only once.

There are a number of key things to remember when writing a report. Firstly, the structure of a psychological research report typically follows the order of Title page, Abstract, Introduction, Method, Results, Discussion, Conclusion, _____ and

_____. The major requirement of the title is that it characterises the _____ report. The report itself should provide a clear, concise _____ of all the major aspects of the _____. It should provide enough detail to allow a reader to find the literature review sources used in the article for themselves and make up their own mind about the interpretation of the results. However, it _____ attempt to give every last detail of the research. The results section of the report should include the _____ of the statistical analysis, but should not include a discussion of the _____ of the results, which should instead be located in the discussion section of the report. However, this structure may not be appropriate for _____ reports, where the findings of the research may be reported while simultaneously linking these findings to extant literature in the field. That is, some qualitative research reports may combine the research _____ section with the _____ section.

Optional items

A. quantitative research

B. results

C. should

D. discussion

E. interpretation

F. research process

G. entire

H. research methodology

I. References

J. should not

K. summary

L. Appendices

M. implications

N. qualitative research

O. findings

P. synthesis

Essay questions for Chapter 11

Once you have completed the MCQs above you are ready to tackle some essay questions. You might like to select three or four topics and make notes on them. One way of doing this is to create a concept map. The first question has been done for you and you can see how the knowledge required links to some of the MCQs in this chapter.

1. Compare and evaluate the methods of reporting quantitative and qualitative research.

2. Describe and discuss the implications of 'publication bias' and suggest potential strategies to overcome this.

3. What are rhetorical strategies and reflexivity, and how are they employed in reporting research? Discuss the implications for both.

4. Critically examine what it means to report research 'ethically'.

5. Compare and contrast the different methods of disseminating research results, such as journal articles and conference presentations, exploring their advantages and disadvantages.

6. Why is it important to consider the ways in which psychological research is reported? Discuss providing examples of research to illustrate your answer.

7. Why is it important to develop and use critical thinking skills when interpreting and conducting research in psychology?

8. Critically examine the issues faced by a researcher when writing an effective research report for publication.

Chapter 11 essay question 1: concept map

Compare and evaluate the methods of reporting quantitative and qualitative research.

The concept map opposite provides an example of how the first sample essay may be conceptualised. Consideration of the different approaches taken by quantitative and qualitative researchers to exploring psychological processes and phenomena reveals several subtopics. Critically evaluating this provides insight into the emphasis placed on reporting statistics, researcher reflexivity and extant theory, for example. Also revealed are differences in the conceptualisation and method of reporting theory generation. Exploring these issues demonstrates an understanding of the implications that different reporting styles have on understanding psychological and social phenomena.

Remember that it is important to link your answers to other topic areas not covered in this chapter.

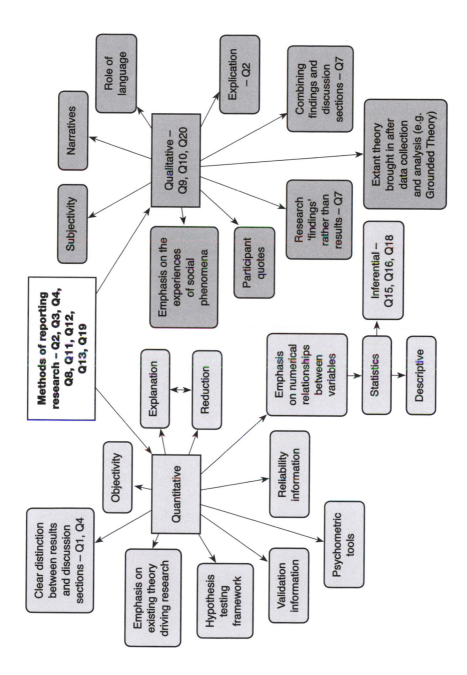

Writing an essay: a format for success

When writing an essay on research methods it is important to remember that psychologists use many different approaches to studying phenomena. This diversity in approaches mostly arises from differences in epistemological and ontological perspectives between the different fields in psychology. For example, research in cognitive psychology may be more associated with the positivist paradigm and therefore quantitative experimental methodology than research in social psychology. However, it is crucial to remember that there are always exceptions, and even within one psychological field researchers will make use of a range of methodologies.

Other factors which affect research design relate to the topic of interest, as some methodologies may be more appropriate for studying a particular issue than others. To write a good essay you need to demonstrate that you recognise the different approaches to research, their strengths and weaknesses, and ultimately the implications these factors have for our understanding of the phenomena under investigation.

When planning an essay you will often need to make a decision about whether an essay requires a broad overview and evaluation of a topic or should focus in more detail on a small number of key concepts. So, make sure you read the question carefully and use your concept maps to develop an essay plan in which all the key issues are covered, the points you make are relevant to the question posed and your argument flows logically from one issue to the next.

To write an essay which really stands out you will need to go beyond merely describing the issue at hand and will instead need to impartially present both sides of an argument, before evaluating these approaches and stating where your position in regard to the argument lies and why. Remember, your position in the debate needs to be based on a critical appraisal of the evidence available rather than on opinion alone. So, provide well-chosen examples of relevant research and theory to support your arguments.

A successful essay is one that presents a well planned, evidenced argument that demonstrates that you are not only aware of important relevant issues, but you can also apply them to real-life psychological research and debates.

Scoring methods in MCQs

Introduction

All assessments need to be reviewed and marked. At your university you will come across a number of formal (often called summative) and informal (aka formative) assessments. These can take the form of practical reports, essays, short-answer questions and (of course) examinations. There are, of course, a number of forms of examinations – short answers, written essays and multiple-choice questions (or MCQs).

MCQs are considered objective assessments, that is answers are unambiguously correct or incorrect and therefore provide for high marker reliability – so that's one positive mark for MCQs. On the other hand, there is often a concern (for the examination setter) that guessing by the candidate can have an inflationary influence on the marks. By chance, if you have four choices then you should score 25% just by guessing. This is obviously not a situation to be encouraged, and because of this your psychology course team may have introduced various attempts to make sure that this does not happen. It is worth exploring some of these methods and the implications these will have for the approach you take to your assessment and, ultimately, how they can impact on your examination performance.

Scoring of MCQ examinations can take several forms. At its most simple, a raw score is calculated based on the total number of correct responses (usually 1 mark per correct answer). Under this approach, any omissions or incorrect responses earn you no marks but neither do they attract a penalty. If you get the question right, you get a mark; if you do not then you get no mark.

As mentioned, alternative and more complex approaches to marking have been developed because of concerns that results can be inflated if correct responses are the result of successful guessing. The most common approaches to discouraging random guessing include the reward of partial knowledge and negative marking. This can impact on your behaviour and your learning. Of course, whatever the examination and whatever the marking scheme, you need to know your stuff!

Rewarding partial knowledge

Scoring procedures developed to reward partial knowledge are based on the assumption that though you and your student colleagues may be unable to identify a single correct response you can confidently identify some options as being incorrect and that partial knowledge should therefore be rewarded. Versions of this approach generally allow you to choose:

- more than one possibly correct response and to be awarded a partial mark provided one of your responses is the correct answer;
- a 'not sure' option for which you are awarded a proportion of a mark (usually either 0.2 or 0.25).

Negative marking

Negative marking is when your performance is based on the total number of correct responses which is then reduced in some way to correct for any potential guessing. The simplest application of negative marking is where equal numbers of marks are added or subtracted for right and wrong answers and omitted answers, or the selection of a 'No answer' option that has no impact on marks. So, you get +1 mark when you get the question right, –1 mark when you get it wrong and 0 if you do not attempt it. However, there are other approaches which are slightly more punitive. In these approaches, if you get the question correct you get +1, if you get the question wrong then this is awarded a –1 (or even –2) and if there is no attempt then this is awarded a –1 as well as, it is suggested, you do not know the answer.

How does this impact on you?

The impact of these scoring mechanisms can be significant. By way of example, use the following table to demonstrate your performance in each of the chapters in this text. For each of the chapters work out the number of correct responses (and code this as NC), the number of incorrect answers (coded as NI) and the number of questions that you did not provide a response to (NR). You can then use the formulae in the table to work out how you would have performed under each of the different marking schemes. For example, for the punitive negative marking scheme you score 18 correct (NC=18), 2 incorrect (NI=2) and omitted 5 questions (NR=5). On the basis of the formula in the table, NC-(NI*2)-NR, you would have scored 9 (i.e. 18-(2*2)-5). So even though you managed to get 18 out of 25 this would have been reduced to only 9 because of the punitive marking.

Chapter	Number correct	Number incorrect	No response	Marking scheme: raw score	Marking scheme: partial knowledge	Marking scheme: negative marking	Marking scheme: punitive negative marking
	NC	NI	NR	= NC	= NC – (NI * 0.2)	= NC – NI	= NC – (NI * 2) – NR
1							
2							
3							
4							
5							
6							
7							
8							
9							
10							
11							
TOTAL							

Explore the scores above – which chapter did you excel at and for which chapter do you need to do some work? Use the above table to see your areas of strength and areas of weakness – and consequently where you need to spend more time revising and reviewing the material.

MCQ answers

Chapter 1: Research in psychology – MCQ answers

Level	Question number	Correct response	Self-monitoring
Foundation	1	D	
Foundation	2	D	
Foundation	3	B	
Foundation	4	D	
Foundation	5	C	
Foundation	6	B	
Foundation	7	A	
Foundation	8	C	
Foundation	9	C	
Foundation	10	C	
Advanced	11	A	
Advanced	12	C	
Advanced	13	A	
Advanced	14	B	
Advanced	15	B	
Advanced	16	A	
Advanced	17	C	
Advanced	18	D	
Advanced	19	B	
Advanced	20	B	
		Total number of points:	Foundation: 3/10 Advanced: 6/10

EMCQ for Chapter 1

The paragraph should read as follows. A maximum of 5 points can be awarded.

Although there is no single 'qualitative approach' to psychological research, many proponents of qualitative approaches argue that traditional quantitative methods conduct research in sterile conditions, often seeking to isolate people from their <u>social contexts</u> in an attempt to ensure that all factors other than those of interest are <u>held constant</u>. This can lead to <u>artificial</u> results and narrow theories, and because traditional quantitative methods seek to reduce social phenomena to <u>numerical relationships</u>, many qualitative researchers argue that they cannot capture the entirety of human experience. Some qualitative researchers also argue that because traditional quantitative methods seek to test hypotheses generated from prior theory rather than <u>generating hypotheses</u> through new research, this may actually stifle the development of new perspectives in psychology.

Chapter 2: Designing research studies – MCQ answers

Level	Question number	Correct response	Self-monitoring
Foundation	1	D	
Foundation	2	B	
Foundation	3	C	
Foundation	4	B	
Foundation	5	A	
Foundation	6	B	
Foundation	7	A	
Foundation	8	C	
Foundation	9	D	
Foundation	10	C	
Advanced	11	A	
Advanced	12	C	
Advanced	13	B	
Advanced	14	A	
Advanced	15	B	
Advanced	16	D	
Advanced	17	C	
Advanced	18	B	
Advanced	19	B	
Advanced	20	D	
		Total number of points:	Foundation: 7/10 Advanced: 3/10

EMCQ for Chapter 2

The paragraph should read as follows. A maximum of 10 points can be awarded.

When designing a research study in psychology a key issue, particularly for <u>quantitative</u> research, is <u>replicability</u>. This refers to the degree to which the results of the study would be found again if the research was repeated. If results are replicated, we can have greater <u>confidence</u> that the psychological effect revealed by the research is <u>real</u>. In order to be able to replicate a piece of research, the <u>full</u> details of the original study are required. This includes ensuring that all the <u>predictions</u>, <u>methods</u> and <u>results</u> obtained in the study are clearly stated in the <u>research report</u>. Otherwise, it is not possible to repeat the research without the risk of severely <u>confounding</u> the research findings, for example through using different procedures or techniques.

Chapter 3: The basics of experimental design – MCQ answers

Level	Question number	Correct response	Self-monitoring
Foundation	1	C	✓
Foundation	2	B	
Foundation	3	D	
Foundation	4	C	
Foundation	5	D	
Foundation	6	D	
Foundation	7	A	
Foundation	8	B	
Foundation	9	A	
Foundation	10	A	
Foundation	11	C	
Advanced	12	A	
Advanced	13	B	
Advanced	14	A	
Advanced	15	C	
Advanced	16	A	
Advanced	17	B	
Advanced	18	A	
Advanced	19	C	
Advanced	20	C	
Advanced	21	A	
Advanced	22	D	
		Total number of points:	Foundation: 9/11 Advanced: 6/10

EMCQ for Chapter 3

The paragraph should read as follows. A maximum of 7 points can be awarded.

There are two types of <u>repeated-measures</u> design, the complete and the incomplete design, which require different techniques to control for <u>practice effects</u>, which are broadly referred to as <u>counterbalancing</u> techniques. A <u>complete</u> design involves ensuring that practice effects are balanced for each participant by administering the conditions to each participant several times using <u>different</u> orders each time. In an <u>incomplete</u> design, however, each condition is administered to each participant <u>only once</u>, and the order of administering the conditions is varied across participants rather than for each participant.

Chapter 4: Designing complex experiments – MCQ answers

Level	Question number	Correct response	Self-monitoring
Foundation	1	B	
Foundation	2	A	
Foundation	3	A	
Foundation	4	D	
Foundation	5	C	
Foundation	6	A	
Foundation	7	B	
Foundation	8	A	
Foundation	9	D	
Foundation	10	C	
Advanced	11	A	
Advanced	12	A	
Advanced	13	B	
Advanced	14	D	
Advanced	15	A	
Advanced	16	A	
Advanced	17	B	
Advanced	18	A	
Advanced	19	D	
Advanced	20	B	
		Total number of points:	Foundation: 6/10 Advanced: 6/10

EMCQ for Chapter 4

The correct statements are as follows. A maximum of 3 points can be awarded.

A. There appears to be an interaction effect between school type and the intervention: secondary school teachers' stress scores appear to have decreased to a greater extent than primary school teachers' stress scores.

E. It is not possible to say whether any differences between pre-test and post-test scores are statistically significant from examining this graph alone.

F. This experiment should be described as a mixed design.

Chapter 5: Case studies, single-case and small-n designs – MCQ answers

Level	Question number	Correct response	Self-monitoring
Foundation	1	C	
Foundation	2	D	
Foundation	3	D	
Foundation	4	A	
Foundation	5	C	
Foundation	6	A	
Foundation	7	B	
Foundation	8	A	
Foundation	9	A	
Foundation	10	D	
Advanced	11	A	
Advanced	12	B	
Advanced	13	A	
Advanced	14	D	
Advanced	15	D	
Advanced	16	A	
Advanced	17	A	
Advanced	18	D	
Advanced	19	D	
Advanced	20	C	
		Total number of points:	Foundation: 4/10 Advanced:

EMCQ for Chapter 5

The paragraphs should read as follows. A maximum of 8 points can be awarded.

Case studies have a number of advantages. Case studies can provide a chance to study <u>rare</u> phenomena, such as patients with prosopagnosia (a disorder of face perception), which it would not be possible to study otherwise. Case studies can be used to <u>challenge</u> theory, for example when the behaviour of a single case contradicts theoretical principles or claims. Alternatively, this type of research can be used to <u>tentatively support</u> a theory, although it should never be taken as conclusive. Finally, case studies are idiographic in nature but can be used to complement <u>nomothetic</u> research, for example in clinical research.

It should also be recognised that the case study method has disadvantages too: the main criticism concerns the inability to make <u>causal inferences</u>, because <u>extraneous</u> variables are not controlled. Also, there is a high risk of <u>observer bias</u> or bias in data collection, which may lead to misleading interpretations of the findings from such research. Lastly, there is also an issue regarding the degree to which research findings can be <u>generalised</u>.

Chapter 6: Observational methods – MCQ answers

Level	Question number	Correct response	Self-monitoring
Foundation	1	C	
Foundation	2	C	
Foundation	3	D	
Foundation	4	D	
Foundation	5	A	
Foundation	6	C	
Foundation	7	D	
Foundation	8	D	
Foundation	9	B	
Foundation	10	B	
Advanced	11	C	
Advanced	12	A	
Advanced	13	D	
Advanced	14	D	
Advanced	15	B	
Advanced	16	A	
Advanced	17	A	
Advanced	18	B	
Advanced	19	C	
Advanced	20	D	
		Total number of points:	Foundation: Advanced:

EMCQ for Chapter 6

The paragraph should read as follows. A maximum of 13 points can be awarded.

Observational research can be both <u>quantitative</u> and <u>qualitative</u> in nature. It is often used in research to overcome the issue of the gap between <u>stated</u> behaviour and <u>actual</u> behaviour and is believed by some researchers to provide a more <u>valid</u> and <u>accurate</u> picture of human behaviour than survey and interview methods. However, it faces a number of criticisms; there is a risk of imposing a potentially <u>irrelevant framework</u>, in the form of a <u>coding scheme</u>, on the behaviour to be observed. However, this could be overcome by running <u>pilot</u> research using <u>unstructured</u> observation to ensure the coding scheme is relevant. Also, some researchers argue that by observing only overt behaviour these methods are unable to capture <u>meaning</u> and <u>intention</u>. Linked to this is the concern that observational research loses sight of the <u>context</u> in which the behaviour occurs and can generate scraps of fragmented information. The difficulty then faced by the researcher is to organise this information in a coherent, accurate and meaningful way.

Chapter 7: Survey research – MCQ answers

Level	Question number	Correct response	Self-monitoring
Foundation	1	D	
Foundation	2	A	
Foundation	3	B	
Foundation	4	D	
Foundation	5	D	
Foundation	6	D	
Foundation	7	C	
Foundation	8	B	
Foundation	9	A	
Foundation	10	C	
Advanced	11	A	
Advanced	12	B	
Advanced	13	D	
Advanced	14	C	
Advanced	15	D	
Advanced	16	A	
Advanced	17	C	
Advanced	18	B	
Advanced	19	C	
Advanced	20	B	
		Total number of points:	Foundation: Advanced:

EMCQ for Chapter 7

The paragraph should read as follows. A maximum of 10 points can be awarded.

Researchers designing a questionnaire can make use of a range of different <u>response scales</u>. The most commonly used in psychological research is the Likert scale (Likert, 1932), also known as the <u>summated ratings</u> scale. This scale involves presenting the participant with a statement, which they are asked to record their attitude toward on a scale comprising an <u>equal</u> number of <u>favourable and unfavourable</u> statements (e.g. strongly agree to strongly disagree). Each possible answer is associated with a unique number, which can then be used to calculate a mean for all items on that scale. The Likert scale is not without controversy, however; many researchers use the data derived from them as <u>interval level</u> data. However, other researchers argue that the data represents <u>ordinal level</u> measurement and therefore is not suitable for the same statistical procedures. Another type of response scale is the <u>semantic differential</u> (Osgood, Suci and Tannenbaum, 1957). These scales are formed so that there are two <u>bipolar adjectives</u> and participants are invited to mark on the space between them where they feel their position toward the attitude object lies. This allows the respondent greater <u>flexibility</u> in expressing how they feel, but is extremely hard to analyse, as different participants' responses are extremely unlikely to be <u>comparable</u>.

Chapter 8: Reliability and validity– MCQ answers

Level	Question number	Correct response	Self-monitoring
Foundation	1	B	
Foundation	2	D	
Foundation	3	B	
Foundation	4	A	
Foundation	5	C	
Foundation	6	B	
Foundation	7	C	
Foundation	8	D	
Foundation	9	C	
Foundation	10	D	
Advanced	11	D	
Advanced	12	C	
Advanced	13	B	
Advanced	14	C	
Advanced	15	B	
Advanced	16	D	
Advanced	17	C	
Advanced	18	B	
Advanced	19	B	
Advanced	20	A	
		Total number of points:	Foundation: 3/10 Advanced: 4/10

EMCQ for Chapter 8

The paragraph should read as follows. A maximum of 14 points can be awarded.

The term 'validity' is often applied in a different way to qualitative psychological research than to quantitative psychological research, owing to epistemological and ontological differences between the two approaches. For this reason Lincoln and Guba (1985) suggest that rather than 'validity', qualitative researchers should explore the degree of 'trustworthiness' of their data. According to these authors, this construct comprises four concepts: confirmability, transferability, credibility, and dependability. Credibility refers to the evaluation of whether or not the findings from research offer a reasonable and plausible interpretation of the data collected. Transferability refers to the degree to which the findings of the research can be applied outside the boundaries of the specific study in question. Dependability refers to the assessment of the quality of the data collection, data analysis and theory generation processes carried out during the research. Finally, confirmability refers to an assessment of the extent to which the research findings are actually supported by the data collected. This approach also highlights the different role that the concept of 'representativeness' plays in qualitative research compared to quantitative research. For example, qualitative research often makes use of the case study method. In this type of research the emphasis is placed on exploring the internal dynamics of the specific individual or organisation selected for the research, rather than attempting to generalise research findings to a wider group of people. Therefore representativeness is not an issue in this situation. However, although qualitative research often employs small, 'unrepresentative' samples, there may be instances in which generalisation of an observed experience is desirable. In these situations qualitative researchers often make use of accumulative techniques, such as checking an experience in one context against similar experiences in other contexts.

Chapter 9: Qualitative approaches and methods – MCQ answers

Level	Question number	Correct response	Self-monitoring
Foundation	1	D	
Foundation	2	B	
Foundation	3	C	
Foundation	4	A	
Foundation	5	C	
Foundation	6	C	
Foundation	7	D	
Foundation	8	A	
Foundation	9	B	
Foundation	10	A	
Advanced	11	D	
Advanced	12	A	
Advanced	13	B	
Advanced	14	A	
Advanced	15	C	
Advanced	16	A	
Advanced	17	B	
Advanced	18	B	
Advanced	19	D	
Advanced	20	C	
		Total number of points:	Foundation: 10 Advanced: 6

$$\frac{16}{20} = \frac{80}{100}\ \%$$

EMCQ for Chapter 9

The paragraph should read as follows. A maximum of 9 points can be awarded.

Hammersley (1966) proposed a classification for approaches to <u>multi-strategy</u> research, and identified three key approaches to research which combines <u>quantitative</u> and <u>qualitative</u> research. The first approach is called <u>triangulation</u>, which refers to the use of quantitative research to <u>corroborate</u> qualitative research findings, or qualitative research to corroborate quantitative research findings. The second approach is called <u>facilitation</u>, which refers to the situation in which one research strategy is employed in order to <u>aid</u> research using the other research strategy. The third approach identified is termed <u>complementarity</u>. This approach is used when two research strategies are employed in order that different aspects of an investigation can be <u>married</u> together.

Chapter 10: Ethics of research with humans and animals – MCQ answers

Level	Question number	Correct response	Self-monitoring
Foundation	1	B	
Foundation	2	B	
Foundation	3	C	
Foundation	4	C	
Foundation	5	D	
Foundation	6	D	
Foundation	7	A	
Foundation	8	B	
Foundation	9	A	
Foundation	10	C	
Advanced	11	C	
Advanced	12	C	
Advanced	13	B	
Advanced	14	B	
Advanced	15	A	
Advanced	16	D	
Advanced	17	C	
Advanced	18	A	
Advanced	19	D	
Advanced	20	B	
		Total number of points:	Foundation: 5/10 Advanced: 3 ⎯ 7

EMCQ for Chapter 10

The paragraphs should read as follows. A maximum of 13 points can be awarded.

The term 'informed consent' refers to the explicit statement of a person's willingness to participate in a research study, which is based on a clear understanding of the nature of the research, who is conducting the research, what the participant can expect if they choose to take part and any consequences they should be aware of if they do not take part. Key information that should be provided includes the fact that participation is voluntary and the participant can withdraw at any time without having to provide a reason. The contact details for the researcher/research team (so that participants can ask further questions about the study) should be provided, as well as information about sources of support should the participant require it and also information about how they can make an official complaint.

There are a number of difficulties which researchers encounter when trying to obtain informed consent. For example, the anonymity of participants and confidentiality of their data must be ensured. Informed consent is also difficult to establish with specific methodologies, such as Internet research (where the researcher cannot be certain that a participant is really of the required age or fully understands the information they have read) and ethnomethodology (where the diverse range of people observed, for example, means that informed consent is difficult to obtain – particularly if employing covert observational methods). Another issue concerns individuals who do not have the capacity to consent to their participation, such as children and vulnerable adults. In these circumstances, researchers may seek to obtain informed consent from the individual's legal guardian, such as a parent. Therefore it is important to recognise that obtaining informed consent is more than a participant deciding to take part in research; it is a reciprocal process whereby the researcher must also be in a position to judge the quality of a potential participant's decision.

Chapter 11: Reporting research – MCQ answers

Level	Question number	Correct response	Self-monitoring
Foundation	1	D	
Foundation	2	C	
Foundation	3	A	
Foundation	4	A	
Foundation	5	B	
Foundation	6	D	
Foundation	7	D	
Foundation	8	A	
Foundation	9	D	
Foundation	10	D	
Advanced	11	A	
Advanced	12	D	
Advanced	13	A	
Advanced	14	C	
Advanced	15	B	
Advanced	16	B	
Advanced	17	D	
Advanced	18	A	
Advanced	19	A	
Advanced	20	C	
		Total number of points:	Foundation: Advanced:

EMCQ *for Chapter* 11

The paragraph should read as follows. A maximum of 11 points can be awarded.

There are a number of key things to remember when writing a report. Firstly, the structure of a psychological research report typically follows the order of Title page, Abstract, Introduction, Method, Results, Discussion, Conclusion, <u>References</u> and <u>Appendices</u>. The major requirement of the title is that it characterises the <u>entire</u> report. The report itself should provide a clear, concise <u>synthesis</u> of all the major aspects of the <u>research process</u>. It should provide enough detail to allow a reader to find the literature review sources used in the article for themselves and make up their own mind about the interpretation of the results. However, it <u>should not</u> attempt to give every last detail of the research. The results section of the report should include the <u>interpretation</u> of the statistical analysis, but should not include a discussion of the <u>implications </u>of the results, which should instead be located in the discussion section of the report. However, this structure may not be appropriate for <u>qualitative research</u> reports, where the findings of the research may be reported while simultaneously linking these findings to extant literature in the field. That is, some qualitative research reports may combine the research <u>findings</u> section with the <u>discussion</u> section.